Elvis Presley
in Hollywood

Overleaf: Emotional conflict and physically violent encounters formed a large part of the earlier films.
LOVING YOU

Elvis Presley
in Hollywood

Celluloid Sell-Out

Gerry McLafferty

ROBERT HALE · LONDON

© *Gerry McLafferty 1989*
First published in Great Britain 1989

Robert Hale Limited
Clerkenwell House
Clerkenwell Green
London EC1R 0HT

British Library Cataloguing in Publication Data

McLafferty, Gerry
  Elvis Presley in Hollywood:
  celluloid sell-out
  1. American cinema films. Acting.
  Presley, Elvis to 1972
  791.43′028′0924

  ISBN 0–7090–3729–9

Photoset in New Century Schoolbook by
Derek Doyle & Associates, Mold, Clwyd.
Printed in Great Britain by
Butler & Tanner Ltd., Frome, Somerset.

Contents

Illustrations

Acknowledgements

The author wishes to thank the following: Bryan Forbes for words of encouragement, my wife Linda for her unswerving faith and Todd Slaughter for his invaluable support. I wish to dedicate this book to the memory of my dear father, John McLafferty.

Grateful acknowledgements are extended to the following for information included in this book:

Me 'N' Elvis by Charlie Hodge with Charles Goodman (Castle Books Inc.)
Elvis: What Happened? by Red West, Sonny West, Dave Hebler as told to Steve Dunleavy (Ballantine Books)
Hollywood in a Suitcase by Sammy Davis jun. (William Collins)
Bruce Lee – King of Kung Fu by Felix Dennis and Don Atyeo (Wildwood House)
Bronson by David Downing (W.H. Allen)
Halliwell's Film Guide (Granada)
Monthly Film Bulletin; Films and Filming; Photoplay; Elvis Monthly; New Musical Express; Reveille; Disc & Music Echo; Glasgow *Evening Times; Radio Times; The Hollywood Reporter; Joe Esposito Productions, Inc.;* BBC Television; BBC Radio

Although every effort has been made to identify copyright holders and obtain their permission, the author and publishers would be glad to hear of any inadvertent error or omissions.

G.M.

Preface

Collectively, Elvis Presley's films are dismissed as little more than technicolour trivia, whilst Elvis Presley himself is ultimately looked upon as a figure of ridicule by the doyens of the cinema world. His importance as a screen personality deserves a deeper understanding. What I have set out to argue is that, when given the correct opportunities, Elvis Presley was an actor of considerable depth. He displayed a powerful, brooding presence on screen, and could bring out an emotional response in an audience.

Few people realize that many of the performers and production staff associated with his Hollywood career were in the category of Academy Award winners or nominees. Gradually, however, a certain stigma was attached to those who were in any way involved with his films, and even people like Martin Scorsese (now a highly successful film director) dissociated himself from his work on *Elvis On Tour*.

Why was Elvis Presley disregarded by the Hollywood élite? Why did he continue with an unworthy film career? Within the pages of this book, an attempt has been made to determine the pros and cons of what was, although financially rewarding, a greatly misguided career.

Elvis Presley died in August 1977, and so without the opportunity of redemption, his films have to stand for what they are. This suggests a form of judgement and, indeed, the media and critics alike have described this important phase of his life, almost without exception, in the harshest terms imaginable.

For a lengthy period in his career, Elvis Presley gave a great deal to Hollywood, which, in turn, failed to reciprocate. He spent sixteen years as a prolific film star in Hollywood, and completed thirty-three motion pictures in that time. The work he has left behind deserves closer attention.

Ina Balin (pictured) was Elvis's co-star in this 1968 revenge western: '... for me it was a marvellous experience working with Elvis, because I think he is an instinctively fine actor ...'.

CHARRO!

1 The Formative Years (1956–58)

I'd like to prove myself as an actor, but I'm still not sure of my ability.

Elvis Presley on film

The Dream Machine that is Hollywood has, in the past, as it still does today, run relatively smoothly in the creation of its 'in-house' stars. The studios vary their methods. The seven-year contract arrangement was very much the order of the day, even for established actors, up until the 1950s. There were exceptions to this pattern, of course, and by the early 1960s individual picture deals were the standard.

The durability of top stars is something again. Today, more than ever, a film star is only as popular as his/her last success. Accordingly, film properties are subject to the 'bankability' of the star, if they are to be made at all. I am not suggesting that this is a hard and fast rule. Far from it. Some of the top ten films of all time featured virtual unknowns, such as *ET*, and the *Star Wars* series. Certainly, as a direct result, Harrison Ford emerged as a fully established leading actor, but up until *Star Wars* he was very much a supporting player. But even present-day stars have their flops, and therefore have to consider future projects most carefully in order to maintain their top status.

In the heyday of Hollywood, top producers were the legendary figures: Louis B. Mayer, Jack Warner, Darryl F. Zanuck, Harry Cohn, Sam Goldwyn, Irving Thalberg (who died tragically aged thirty-seven, and on whom F. Scott Fitzgerald allegedly based his unfinished book *The Last Tycoon*). They were famed for their enormous houses, arrays

15

of beautiful women, vast spending on outrageously lavish parties and, perhaps above all, famed for the fear they put into the hearts of everyone within the industry, from leading players down to film-set minions – a fear engendered by their penchant for firing at will any nonconformists. They did have awesome power and invariably used that power to its utmost. They had almost total control, a dangerous commodity in any industry, and one which, I feel, was harmful to the film business, because commercial viability took precedence over any artistic considerations. If film was art, then that was fine – as long as it was profitable.

A number of actors have taken up the quest for personal creative fulfilment, diversifying from expected characterizations. Alas, it has almost always had disastrous results. In 1977, after a four-year self-imposed break from film work, the late Steve McQueen, in a fit of self-indulgence, starred in a screen version of the Henrik Ibsen classic *An Enemy of the People*. The film sank without trace, in fact remaining unreleased in most countries. An all but unrecognizable McQueen, as the spurned doctor, gave an admirable performance – but cinema audiences only wanted to see him as a man of action. He was typecast, and the Ibsen story, I would say, was his way of rebelling against his own image. Individual attempts at cinematic iconoclasm are rarely, if ever, successful.

To a lesser degree this also happened to Clint Eastwood, although fortunately for him, he rectified this 'error' with his next project. In 1982, he starred in and directed *Honkytonk Man*, a gentle story, with a fair smattering of pathos, about a dying country singer. It had some nice humorous touches and an able supporting cast, but obviously it was so out of character for Eastwood that audiences found the idea unacceptable. As with the story's central character, the film died upon its release in the United States and in the UK it was denied a cinematic release altogether – the only Eastwood film to date that has suffered this fate since he came to prominence in the late 1960s. In his next film, *Sudden Impact*, he returned to the familiar ground of his Dirty Harry character. This proved to be an enormous success and his previous 'misdemeanour' was forgiven.

No matter how loyal an audience might seem, it would appear that the golden rule is: Do not deviate too far from characterizations that people expect from you. To be typecast can be a very successful, long-lasting and financially rewarding formula. It can also have great disadvantages. This was exactly the problem with Hollywood and Elvis Presley.

Legend has it that producer Hal B. Wallis saw Elvis Presley on television in 1956, decided that he had a definite presence, and should promptly be tested as a motion picture actor. The pedigree was good. After all, it was Wallis who had been responsible for discovering some of the now famous names – among them, Burt Lancaster, Errol Flynn and Humphrey Bogart. Wallis was also instrumental in the transition from stage to screen of the Dean Martin–Jerry Lewis double act.

So, the helmsman was appointed. Wallis galvanized his crew into action. Firstly, the screen test was arranged. This would hopefully enable the studios to ascertain the true potential of Elvis Presley's embryonic talent. At that time, in April 1956, Wallis was producing *The Rainmaker* which starred Burt Lancaster and Katharine Hepburn. Elvis's test featured him performing, with supporting actor Frank Faylen, the role in the film which was taken by Earl Holliman – that of the hothead younger brother of Miss Hepburn. Some confusion exists over this test as, at one point, Elvis himself announced that *The Rainmaker* was in fact to be his film début. In an interview in 1956 he made that very statement. However, this was not the case. His only association with the film was his screen test. It would appear that a certain success could be attributed to the test, as Elvis was signed to a seven-year contract by Paramount Pictures.

Love Me Tender

Love Me Tender, made in 1956, marked Elvis's rather surprising but auspicious film début. Surprising because no one expected to first see him in a tense Civil War drama. Whilst there are no definite rules, aspiring singers who transfer to the screen are usually cast in a musical — certainly to begin with. Unlike his subsequent films, *Love Me Tender* was not designed as a vehicle specifically for Elvis. Indeed, he was third-billed, after Richard Egan and Debra Paget — both popular players of the 1950s. The production began shooting under the title of *The Reno Brothers*, since it concerned four brothers, of whom Elvis was the youngest, Clint. Richard Egan was the strong eldest brother, Vance, and James Drury and William Campbell completed the Reno quartet. Part way through the production it was decided to change the title to *Love Me Tender*, for obvious commercial reasons. The title song was very popular and this change would almost certainly guarantee longer queues at the box-office. Looking back, I wonder how the other actors and production staff viewed this alteration? After all, the finished title hardly suggests an action drama, steeped in Civil War tension. To be fair, much of the plot concerned bitter conflict within the romantic triangle involving the three main characters; therefore the studio obviously felt their decision was justified.

The film was directed by Robert D. Webb and produced by David Weisbart, who had also produced the cultist *Rebel Without a Cause*, starring James Dean, in 1955. Weisbart went on to produce a further three Elvis Presley films. The screenplay was written by Robert Buckner, and was based on a story by Maurice Geraghty.

In the story, Elvis as Clint Reno, is at home while his three brothers are involved in the bitter fighting of the Civil War. When the three battle-weary brothers return, the family is shocked to find that eldest brother Vance is still alive, for they had been informed that he had been killed. In his

Previous page: The first screen appearance. An off-set hat adjustment by co-star Debra Paget. Richard Egan (left) and James Drury look on. LOVE ME TENDER

20

A tense confrontation between brothers. William Campbell is menacing whilst Debra Paget displays concern. The Civil War setting was a surprising choice for Elvis's screen debut.
LOVE ME TENDER

absence Clint has married Cathy, Vance's sweetheart, and it soon becomes obvious that her feelings for the latter are as strong as ever before.

The situation worsens when the brothers are arrested for their part in an army payroll hold-up. They promptly escape, with the help of former colleagues, and are now on the run.

Clint's jealousy over Cathy and Vance becomes obsessive, and he is easily led to believe that they are planning to go

21

away together. He confronts and assaults Cathy, and demands to know where Vance is hiding out.

When Clint and Vance's former colleagues arrive at the hide-out, a gun battle ensues, and in a blind rage, Clint shoots Vance, before being fatally wounded himself. Vance recovers, and the story ends with the burial of Clint.

The music for the film comprised four songs, one of which was the title song. All of them are credited as having been written by Vera Matson and Elvis Presley, but this was purely a contractual arrangement, and Elvis in fact did not compose any of the songs. They were all written by Ken Darby, Vera Matson's husband, who was credited on the film with 'Vocal Supervision'.

In his very first acting performance, Elvis came across reasonably well. There were moments when his inexperience was evident but, overall, his efforts were commendable. There have been other greatly inferior film débuts.

Elvis, as mentioned before, had signed a seven-year contract with Paramount Pictures in 1956, under the guidance of Hal Wallis. However, not having an immediate property ready, Wallis 'loaned' him to 20th Century Fox for *Love Me Tender*. Elvis went on to make two further dramatic films for that studio upon completion of his military service.

Loving You

In early 1957 shooting began on *Loving You*, which was directed by Hal Kanter, who also co-wrote the screenplay with Herbert Baker, from a story by Mary Agnes Thompson. Hal Wallis was on hand in his first assignment as producer on an Elvis Presley film. His co-stars in the film were Wendell Corey and Lizabeth Scott, both players of some merit. Coincidentally, Corey had featured in the previous year's *The Rainmaker* – the film on which Elvis had undertaken his screen test. Dolores Hart, in her first of two films with Elvis, played Susan, the love interest in the story.

The plot has Elvis as the surly Deke Rivers, who, due to the shrewd dealings of a sharp entrepreneur, Glenda Markle (Lizabeth Scott), finds himself on the road, singing with a country band. Deke's style of music is far removed from country, and he meets with strong disapproval from the band's leader (Wendell Corey).

Deke is attracted to the much older Glenda who encourages him initially, then rebuffs him at a time when he is on the threshold of major success. The emotional Deke runs away from it all, only to return at the last moment when he is to tape a television appearance. He realizes his folly, and his identity crisis is over. It is Susan he truly loves.

The music in the film is raw and exciting. Visually, it was put over extremely well, giving cinema-goers the first real opportunity to witness the unique stage performance of Elvis Presley. At twenty-two years of age, Elvis was vibrant and extremely physical in his performance, and in the film, displays clear examples of his ability. The sound-track featured classic songs like 'Teddy Bear', 'Mean Woman Blues', and 'Lonesome Cowboy'. Overall, it was an excellent soundtrack, and still stands up very well today.

By the time Elvis started this his second film, the famous jet-black hair adorned his head. His own much lighter hair had been seen (albeit in monochrome) in *Love Me Tender* and was only ever seen again in two of his three films for the

United Artists company, namely *Follow That Dream* and *Kid Galahad*. He wore a (very obvious) blond wig in *Kissin' Cousins* of course, but other than on these occasions, he continued with the dyed black hair look for his whole film career, and indeed beyond, until the time of his death.

The semi-biographical *Loving You* was rather well chosen as his first full starring feature. The parallel with his own career was obvious: small-town truck driver is plucked from obscurity and after some misadventures and stormy times, makes it to go on to the Big Time. Elvis's characterizations in his pre-army films were aggressive and rebellious – filled with underlying menace. This, in a sense, seemed a natural

Veteran actress Lizabeth Scott, from a *film noir* background, played the older woman to Elvis's volatile character – a man confused over his own identity.

LOVING YOU

progression from his stage image – after all, if American parents were shocked and outraged by his overtly suggestive gyrations as a stage performer, then why shouldn't they be upon his transition to the silver screen? Strangely, and despite the fact that this brooding persona seemed natural to Elvis, the studio decided that a change was necessary. When he resumed his film career in 1960 after demobilization from the army, Elvis became, with little more than three exceptions I can note, the all-American nice guy in twenty-five more feature films.

Jailhouse Rock

Before any decidedly artistic decline began in Elvis Presley's screen career, he made two more films which quite clearly displayed his inherent aggression.

The first was MGM's *Jailhouse Rock*, on which work commenced in the spring of 1957. This vehicle gave us Elvis as a brash, pushy and distinctly undesirable character.

The film was directed by Richard Thorpe, who was to work with Elvis again on one further occasion, that being *Fun in Acapulco* in 1963. Thorpe was the director responsible for such films as *Ivanhoe* and *The Great Caruso* in the early 1950s.

The producer of *Jailhouse Rock* was Pandro S. Berman, who had begun in production in the early 1930s, working on films like *The Gay Divorcee* (1934) and *Top Hat* (1935) – both starring vehicles for the legendary dancing team of Fred Astaire and Ginger Rogers. Berman also produced the musical *Ziegfeld Girl* (1941) and in 1955 he worked on *The Blackboard Jungle*, another film concerning teenage anxiety. The screenplay was written by Guy Trosper, from a story by Ned Young.

The co-stars in the film represented a cross-section of Hollywood casting. Judy Tyler, who died in a tragic car crash soon after the film's completion, played Peggy Van Alden, a public relations dealer for a record company. Mickey Shaughnessy played the appropriately-named Hunk Houghton, a veteran country singer who befriends Elvis in the penitentiary, encouraging him to become a singer. Dean Jones, later to become a fully-fledged Walt Disney star in his own right, had a small role as disc jockey Teddy Talbot.

Elvis's own musicians, guitarist Scotty Moore, bass player Bill Black and drummer D.J. Fontana all appeared in the film. The trio had already been seen on screen, as part of the Country band in Elvis's previous film, *Loving You*.

Mike Stoller, who, with his partner Jerry Leiber, co-wrote most of the songs featured in the film, also appeared in the film as a piano player.

In the story Elvis is cast as Vince Everett, who, after serving eighteen months in the penitentiary for manslaughter, embarks upon a singing career. He is greatly inspired in this goal by his opportunistic former cell-mate, now a washed-up country singer. He has a fortuitous meeting with a promotions girl from a record company, Peggy (Judy Tyler) and they form a serious, but distant, business relationship.

Following a degree of failure in showbusiness, Vince finally becomes a major success, even venturing as far as making films. He unrelentingly uses and abuses everyone in his quest for stardom, and falls foul of the tempestuous Hunk, who beats him with such force that he causes severe damage to Vince's larynx.

After a life-saving operation and a genuine request for forgiveness from a remorseful Hunk, Vince realizes that his vocal chords are intact, and with this wonderful news he embraces Peggy. They are both very much in love.

Elvis's excellent portrayal of a totally ruthless, exploitative person was the indispensable backbone of the film. It is *difficult to like* his character, and that, in itself, is the entire essence: it surely tells us that the actor has been convincing. If you can leave a cinema saying, 'What a bastard *he* was!', then that person, that actor, has left an indelible mark on you.

Producer Pandro S. Berman said in a radio interview some years ago that when he was assigned to do the film, he was informed by the studio that the sole priority was profit – no real artistic considerations. It is a great credit to Elvis Presley that his performance in the film left this cynical studio greed very much in the shade.

The musical sequences, three decades later, seem not to have dated at all – the songs are still fresh and exciting. The single release of 'Jailhouse Rock'/'Treat Me Nice' reached Number One in the charts in February 1958. The title song sequence, with the mock prison set, is perhaps the most visually exhilarating of all the scores in Elvis Presley's films. According to the television documentary 'Heroes of Rock 'n' Roll', which was presented by the actor Jeff Bridges, Elvis

Elvis himself choreographed the energetic and
visually exciting 'Jailhouse Rock' song sequence but
this fact was strangely excluded from the credits.
JAILHOUSE ROCK

28

The exploitative ex-convict has his first encounter
with Judy Tyler, who selflessly guides him to fame
and fortune.
JAILHOUSE ROCK

himself did the choreography for the title song sequence. Yet, if this is true, why the mysterious omission of such relevant information on the film's credits?

There has been little or no information to suggest that Elvis was ever involved in arranging or choreographing dance sequences in any of his other films. The late Charles O'Curran was credited on several productions as musical numbers arranger.

Jailhouse Rock was Elvis Presley's first feature for MGM. He went on to star in a total of fourteen for that company, but this début film for them was the only one with a serious nature. Discounting the two documentaries made by them, the remaining films were mostly light-hearted affairs, and posed no threat to any contenders in the Academy Award stakes.

King Creole

King Creole, Elvis's fourth film (and his last to be shot in black and white) was the only one completed in 1958. In fact, it almost wasn't. Elvis had received his call-up papers, but since pre-production work had already begun on the film, Paramount Studios were apparently in a panic due to the financial outlay already undertaken for the project. At their request, Elvis personally wrote to the draft board, asking for a three-month deferment, in order that both he and Paramount could fulfil their obligations. The request was granted, much to the relief of the studio. Elvis completed the movie, then promptly attired himself in military uniform. It was to be more than two years before he would set foot in a film studio again – with a whole new image.

The director of *King Creole* was Michael Curtiz, Hal Wallis produced, and the screenplay was written by Herbert Baker and Michael Vincente Gazzo.

Elvis's co-stars were of a high calibre. As the vicious Maxie Fields, Walter Matthau excelled in what was an uncharacteristic performance. Matthau went on to become a major leading player himself, staying mainly in comedy. He won an Academy Award as best supporting actor for the 1966 film *The Fortune Cookie* (UK title: *Meet Whiplash Willie*), his first screen pairing with Jack Lemmon.

In the BBC documentary *Presley* screened in 1987 Walter Matthau spoke of his association with Elvis on the film:

> I almost hesitate, I creep up to the sentence – he was an instinctive actor. That almost is a derogation of his talents. That's saying, well you know he's just a dumb animal who does it well by instinct. No, he was quite bright too. He was very intelligent.
>
> Also, he was intelligent enough to understand what a character was, and how to play the character simply by being himself through the means of the story.
>
> Michael Curtiz used to call him Elvy and he'd call me Valty.

31

He'd say 'Now Elvy and Valty come here [Matthau impersonating Curtiz's broken English], now Valty this is not Academy Award scene. Don't act so much. You are high price actor. Make believe you are low price actor. Let Elvy act.' But Elvy didn't *over*act.

He was not a punk. He was very elegant, sedate ... and ... refined and sophisticated.

Vic Morrow, as would-be gangster Shark, gave a solid performance, and helped to establish the turbulent atmosphere of the film. Morrow was a very proficient character actor who endured lasting success until his controversial death, on the set of John Landis's *The Twilight Zone* in 1982.

Veteran character actor Dean Jagger played Elvis's meek father in the film. His career began on stage, after which he moved into films, establishing a niche for himself as a reliable supporting player. In 1949 he won an Academy Award as best supporting actor for his role in Henry King's *Twelve O'Clock High*.

Carolyn Jones was splendid as Ronnie, the reluctant 'moll' of the piece. She had appeared in several notable films of the 1950s, including Fritz Lang's *The Big Heat* (1953); Billy Wilder's *The Seven Year Itch* (1955); and Don Siegel's *Invasion of The Body Snatchers* (1956). The year before *King Creole*, Carolyn Jones was nominated for an Academy Award for her performance in Delbert Mann's *The Bachelor Party*.

In a small role as Sal, one of the gang members, was one Brian Hutton. Over a decade later, he turned to directing as Brian G. Hutton, and among the films he directed were two hugely successful Clint Eastwood war films – *Where Eagles Dare* (1969) and *Kelly's Heroes* (1970).

In the story, Elvis is the belligerent, mixed-up Danny Fisher – a young man beset with increasing emotional problems, both at home and at high school. To supplement his family income (the family consisting of his widowed father and a sister) he works as a helper at a local nightclub. Whilst engaged in this endeavour, he meets Ronnie (Carolyn Jones), who is the 'property' of nightclub owner racketeer Maxie Fields (Walter Matthau), whose jealousy results in a violent, unprovoked attack on Danny's mild-mannered father (Dean Jagger).

Under pressure from Fields, and with great reluctance, circumstances push Danny further and further into the world of crime, until finally he explodes into a violent confrontation with Fields and his cohorts.

Along the way, he falls for Nellie (Dolores Hart), a shy young girl who is unsure of his intentions. The opportunity to become a successful singer in Dixieland music is given to Danny by rival nightclub owner Charlie Legrand (Paul Stewart), and his obvious talent assures a certain future in this area.

Following a chase by vengeance-seeking criminals, Danny kills gang leader Shark (Vic Morrow) and is himself badly wounded. Ronnie finds him and takes him to a secret hideaway, only to be shot herself by the murderous Maxie Fields. She dies in Danny's arms, after which Fields is taken care of and Danny reunited with his family and Nellie.

The music in *King Creole* was absolutely first-rate – a careful blend of rock 'n' roll and Dixieland jazz, producing an immensely pleasurable soundtrack.

Two singles were released from the film, comprising 'Hard Headed Woman'/'Don't Ask Me Why' and 'King Creole'/ 'Dixieland Rock'. In July 1958 the first release reached number two in the charts, and in October the second single climbed as high as number three. The soundtrack, as an entirety, was a gutsy example of Elvis at his very best, and included the classic 'Trouble' – a song rivetingly performed in the film.

The progress in Elvis's acting was more than evident in *King Creole*. His performance seemed far more professional than in his three preceding features. In the company of such motion picture luminaries as Walter Matthau, Vic Morrow and Dean Jagger, Elvis very much held his own.

The film was based on Harold Robbins' *A Stone for Danny Fisher*, but with the exception of some character names and a few incidents, it bore little resemblance to the novel. The book, set in New York, had Danny struggling to be a boxer, whereas *King Creole* was staged in New Orleans (which is of

course the nucleus of Dixieland jazz, and this featured very heavily on the music score), and the goal here was vocal, rather than pugilistic, success. That said, however, the pugnacious attitude of the character was certainly retained, as many fight scenes were featured in the film – the most convincing being the vicious back-alley knife-fight between Danny and Shark.

The film's director, Hungarian-born Michael Curtiz, was then almost at the close of his long and illustrious career (which had begun way back in 1912 when he had directed films in his native Hungary). His many successful films had incuded the thirties and forties classics, *The Charge of the Light Brigade*, with Errol Flynn; *Angels with Dirty Faces*, with James Cagney; and *Casablanca* with Humphrey Bogart, for which Curtiz had won an Academy Award.

It must have seemed a strange departure for him to be involved in what was essentially a musical drama – very much designed as a vehicle for Elvis Presley. He had, of course, directed Kirk Douglas in *Young Man with a Horn* (UK title: *Young Man of Music*) in 1950, and the re-make of *The Jazz Singer* in 1953.

Producer Hal B. Wallis had worked on two of these earlier films with Michael Curtiz so he would have been very familiar with the director's working technique. Both these men were relatively old in 1958, and considering that the intended appeal of the film had to be mostly for the teenage market, then any artistic motivation on their part would seem questionable.

Critics praised Elvis's performance in *King Creole*, stating that he was effectively establishing himself as a motion picture actor. At the age of twenty-three, Elvis must surely have been delighted with these reports. In interviews at that time, he made it abundantly clear that his greatest wish was to be a successful actor. I do believe that he did have a genuine and sincere desire to reach that goal, but with the post-army change in his screen image – hugely successful financially, but wholly detrimental to any progress in his personal ambition – he was hindered enormously.

Perhaps what Elvis lacked at that time was a guiding

Dolores Hart returned for a second screen appearance with Elvis. She was later to leave showbusiness behind her and become a nun.
KING CREOLE

influence within the film industry. Natalie Wood, on the BBC 'Pebble Mill' programme, shortly before her death in 1981, spoke about her association with Elvis back in 1957, when many headlines were made out of their heady, albeit brief, relationship. Miss Wood felt that he had great potential talent as an actor and, had he been under the wing of someone like Elia Kazan, he could have developed a successful dramatic film career. She was probably correct about this, because in the few meaningful scripts Elvis was given, his presence on screen was almost tangible – making an audience overlook, perhaps completely forget, his musical origins.

In the BBC's 1987 'Presley' documentary, songwriter Jerry Leiber echoed the comments of Natalie Wood when he said:

> We [indicating himself and partner Mike Stoller] were talking about a possibility of a project with Elvis Presley, and what we wanted to do was the Nelson Algren book *A Walk on the Wild Side*. And I understood that [Elia] Kazan had evidenced some interest in it and thought that Presley was a raw talent that could be a real comer, you know, a sort of a raw version of a James Dean type. And we got very excited about it, and we got a stone wall ... and not only that, a scolding. They warned us, that if we ever started thinking again in that direction – trying to turn Elvis into some kind of artiste, whatever – and not letting him be who he was, that we wouldn't be working for him very long.

Unfortunately, the only mentor around Elvis was Colonel Tom Parker, who made deal after deal involving both Elvis's recording and screen career. His aim, admirable in itself, was to keep Elvis at the top. However, if the now famous story about Parker receiving fifty per cent of Elvis's income were true, then just think what it was doing for his bank balance. The quality of the subject matter seemed of little importance to the Colonel. Sadly, and inexplicably, Elvis himself appeared to accept the situation.

As late as June 1972, when in fact Elvis's acting career had ended, in a press interview at the Hilton Hotel in New York, Elvis stated that they were at that time 'looking around for a

A seemingly reticent bus boy (waiter) about to prove that he is unconcerned by gangster threats – the famous 'Trouble' sequence in a mob-owned nightclub.
KING CREOLE

good script'. Maybe this was simply fodder for the media; it could just have been a need to express a personal desire for what Elvis may have considered an unfulfilled ambition. Regardless of the reason, it was never to happen. Without the opportunity for redemption, Elvis's prolific, yet shallow, screen career is open to constant critical abuse. This may be deservedly so in part, but it unfairly overlooks the excellent work he produced in the minority of his films.

I would say that there is not a leading actor around who

37

has not appeared in some dreadful films in his career. Take, for example, Michael Caine in *The Swarm*, *Beyond the Poseidon Adventure*, and *The Hand*; think also of Burt Reynolds in *Nickelodeon*, *Lucky Lady* and *At Long Last Love*; and there are many other examples of extremely forgettable films made by leading Hollywood players. Lewis Milestone's 1962 version of *Mutiny on the Bounty* almost broke MGM as a film studio, despite having Marlon Brando as the main star.

King Creole remains one of Elvis's best films, and is undoubtedly one of his most superior performances. If similar roles had continued upon his return to the screen in 1960, then he would have become an extremely accomplished actor. Alas, this was not the case, and Elvis's approach to film-making became increasingly apathetic.

2 Dramatic Challenges (1960–61)

I don't claim to know much about making movies. I leave the decisions to people who do. As for the fact that the script of *Flaming Star* was written with Brando in mind, I'm glad they thought I could do a part designed for such a fine actor.

Elvis Presley on film

GI Blues

With the resumption of Elvis's career after his army service, there seemed a reluctance to shed the military uniform once and for all. Only weeks following his return from Germany to the United States, Elvis appeared on the Frank Sinatra/ Timex-sponsored TV show 'Welcome Home Elvis'. In the opening spot, an obviously nervous Elvis walked on stage in full dress uniform and sang, along with the rest of the gathered guests, the appropriate 'It's Nice to Go Travelling'. At this point, there were several jibes about his army days (for example, Joey Bishop – 'Where the heck are his sideburns?'). All harmless stuff in itself, but it was as if there were a real need to display to prime-time American viewers that 'this boy' had done his bit for his country. To be fair to Elvis, this was perfectly true. Never once had he complained about being drafted, or that his lengthy absence from showbusiness might conceivably end his career forever. He could apparently have opted for the Special Services, whereby as an entertainer, he would have had a much easier time, travelling the world, performing concerts for the forces. Elvis, however, chose not to do this – he wished to perform his duties in exactly the same way as any other draftee, and expected no preferential treatment.

Following a return to the recording studios, and the Sinatra show, Elvis went back to Hollywood in late April 1960 to film *GI Blues*.

The director was Norman Taurog, the man who was to work on more Elvis Presley films than any other director. This was his first Presley feature, and over a period of eight years, he would direct a total of nine. Hal Wallis produced, and the screenplay was written by Edmund Beloin and Henry Garson.

Elvis's leading lady was Juliet Prowse, who proved to be a formidable partner. Her presence was very strong, and greatly overshadowed many of Elvis's future leading ladies.

In the story Elvis is cast as Tulsa MacLean, a member of the 'Pretty Boy II', a US tank unit stationed in Germany (*déjà vu?*). With two buddies (Robert Ivers and James Douglas) he also fronts an aspiring combo. They become involved in a wager situation, and Tulsa is chosen as the one who must attempt to spend a night alone with Lili, a sultry dancer who captivates military and civilian males at the Café Europa nightspot. (*Café Europa* was in fact the title of the film in several European countries).

Tulsa discovers that he is becoming emotionally drawn to Lili and to avoid any distress, he discontinues their relationship. His army friends feel let down by him, but are overjoyed when he does in fact stay at her apartment for a full night. The circumstances of this situation are completely innocent (they are, in fact, babysitting) and have no connection with the wager. The soldiers, however, view it differently, and all bets are paid.

When Lili is made aware of this deception (as she sees it), she is naturally furious with Tulsa. However, when she is informed of his genuine reasons for being with her, she immediately forgives him. They are both very much in love, and decide to get married.

The music in the film was of exemplary standard – a wide choice of material appropriately befitting the film's theme. The title song and another, 'Didja Ever' had an astonishingly commercial-sounding military beat. The single release from the film was 'Wooden Heart'/'Tonight is so Right for Love', and this record made the number one spot in March 1961.

A curiosity regarding the music was the fact that two completely different songs appeared in separate versions of the film. In the English-speaking version, Elvis sang 'Tonight is so Right for Love', and for foreign release a song called 'Tonight's All Right for Love' was the replacement. The reason for this change was due to a copyright problem.

A humorous moment occurs in the film when Elvis is singing with the combo and an uninterested soldier (Ken Becker) inserts a coin in the juke box. We then see a close-up of his choice – 'Blue Suede Shoes' by Elvis Presley. This results in both he and Elvis having a fist fight, but not before he remarks, 'I want to hear the original'. It is interesting to note that, even at this early stage, Elvis was quite willing to poke fun at his own image.

The soundtrack album, as a whole, was first-class, and won a well-deserved Gold Award.

There is not one moment in the film where Elvis is seen *sans* uniform (I think we can safely discount the shower scene). The formula worked very well. This film laid a solid foundation for the stereotypical pattern that was to continue through to 1967, with lasting, damaging consequences. That said, however, *GI Blues* was an extremely entertaining film. The music score was first-rate; the supporting cast was excellent (an especially fine performance by Arch Johnson as the harassed sergeant), and into his somewhat roguish role Elvis fitted quite nicely.

Some filming had already been done in Germany, but without Elvis's participation, due to his military commitments. A very noticeable double was used for these European scenes, a problem which was to become even worse, and quite inexcusable in later films.

A rather amusing anecdote from the time informs us that, immediately before Elvis left Germany, Colonel Parker had fake newspapers printed, with the emblazoned headlines 'ELVIS RE-ENLISTS'. These he promptly despatched to producer Hal Wallis who almost collapsed with fright when he saw

41

A stylish musical
heralding the advent of
the 'family appeal' image.
The rebellious
characterizations of
previous films were about
to disappear.
GI BLUES

The plot was carefully constructed around a tank unit stationed in Germany. Elvis had just ended his two-year military service in Germany, although the story did not reflect his army career overseas. The rugged Arch Johnson (right) was superb as the exasperated sergeant.
GI BLUES

them. So much time and finance had been laid out on *GI Blues* prior to Elvis's actual shooting in Hollywood, that it would have caused a considerable furore with Paramount Studios, had Parker's sensational 'news' been true.

For some inexplicable reason, upon the film's re-release in 1974, and in subsequent TV screenings, Elvis was listed in the cast as Tulsa *McCauley*, when in fact the character he played was called Tulsa *MacLean*.

One point that has often struck me about this film – considering that this was quite carefully designed as the first 'family appeal' Elvis Presley movie, and indeed carried a U Certificate – was that the central theme of the story has undeniably questionable morals. The wager in the plot, to see if Elvis could spend an entire night alone with Juliet Prowse, has to be considered realistically. In spending a night at her flat, what were they supposed to be doing? What, indeed, would a cinema audience of 1960 *expect* them to be doing? Playing cards? I hardly think so. This 'indelicacy' was, in fact, earlier evidenced in *King Creole* when Elvis, as Danny Fisher, takes the innocent Dolores Hart to a seedy hotel under the pretext that he has been invited to a party there. He even gives her a false name and calls himself 'George'. Upon realizing that she wants no part of this crude seduction, and feeling rather ashamed of his attempted deception, he states, 'I'm sorry but I thought you knew the score'. I think the character's intentions were rather obvious and decidedly less than honourable. None of these given examples could be considered shocking or explicit in any form – far from it; but with *GI Blues* particularly, it was a strange choice of story with which to initiate a 'family' image. However, the film was hugely successful and firmly re-established Elvis as a leading box-office attraction.

The true measure of an actor's box-office appeal is seen in the *Motion Picture Herald*'s annual poll of Film Exhibitors – their own top ten stars of the movies. Elvis had only previously figured in their charts in 1957 at number four, after Rock Hudson, John Wayne and, curiously, Pat Boone. His protracted absence from Hollywood during army service was no doubt responsible for his non-appearance in those charts from 1958–1960 but he was placed again in each successive year from 1961–1966, peaking at number five in 1962. This was of course during his most prolific film-making period. Alas, after 1966, with a new dawn in Hollywood and a new breed of stars on the horizon, Elvis was never again to figure in this all-important star chart.

In *GI Blues* Elvis was very smooth and proficient. His transition from rebellious individual to cheerful extrovert was highly professional. With the success of the film, this type of characterization inevitably became the blueprint for future projects. If only Elvis had insisted on acquiring dramatic scripts as well as light-hearted properties, then perhaps the decline in his film career might never have occurred.

Flaming Star

In August 1960 Elvis began work on what proved to be his best film and most praised performance, *Flaming Star*. This turbulent tale of the Old West was a violent study of racial tension, in many ways ahead of its time.

Flaming Star was Elvis Presley's one true cinematic triumph. His portrayal of an immensely violent half-breed Indian was powerfully compelling. In this role in particular, a riveting *tour de force*, Elvis Presley was not a singer attempting a serious screen characterization, rather an explosive *actor* who commanded the entire atmosphere of the film.

The film was said to be intended as a vehicle for Marlon Brando, who was arguably too old for the role at that time. Despite the glowing reputation Brando had as an actor, Elvis Presley was so outstanding in this film, that it would have been difficult for Brando to have bettered or even matched his performance.

Almost everyone connected with *Flaming Star* was of sterling quality. The director was the enormously talented Don Siegel, whose career in films began in the 1930s when he worked as a film librarian and assistant editor for Warner Brothers. His future as a fully-fledged film director started in the late 1940s and a decade later he had to his credit several classic films including *Riot in Cell Block Eleven* (1954) and *Invasion of the Body Snatchers* (1956), his homage to the science fiction genre.

After *Flaming Star*, as well as going on to direct many excellent films, Siegel developed a fairly long association with Clint Eastwood, working with him in no less than six films, the most successful of which was the cultist *Dirty Harry* (1971). Elvis Presley never had a more capable director than Don Siegel.

David Weisbart here produced his second Elvis film, and the screenplay was written by Clair Huffaker and Nunnally Johnson from Huffaker's own novel *Flaming Lance*.

Nunnally Johnson was a gifted screenwriter, producer and director who had an uncanny ability to transfer other people's work (novels, plays and stories) into polished screenplays. He had worked for some of the legendary directors including Fritz Lang and John Ford. With the latter he worked on three films including the classic *The Grapes of Wrath* (1940) – the famous John Steinbeck novel, for the screen adaptation of which Johnson was nominated for an Academy Award. He was also producer on that film.

The changes made from novel to screenplay actually enhanced the film. Flaming Lance was the name of the family ranch in the book and the Black Star of Death formed the elegiac theme of the story. This was a sign that Kiowa Indians could see in the sky as they neared death. It was their own way of realizing that their time had come. In the film it was changed to the Flaming Star of Death.

The co-stars in the film, like the production staff, were a highly proficient crew. Dolores del Rio, the stunning Mexican actress, came out of a self-imposed retirement to play Elvis's Indian mother. She had appeared in many westerns over the years working with directors of the calibre of Raoul Walsh and John Ford.

Steve Forrest as Elvis's strong elder brother was equally convincing in his role. He has proved to be a durable actor in both films and on television over the years. Barbara Eden provided the female interest and although not exactly superfluous, she did take a back seat to the dramatic action in the plot.

Veteran actor John McIntire conveyed a sensitive frontiersman approach in his role as Elvis's father. He has appeared in several notable films, among them Anthony Mann's *Winchester '73* (1950); Robert Aldrich's *Apache* (1954); Richard Brooks's *Elmer Gantry* (1960); and Alfred Hitchcock's *Psycho* (1960). He was still active in films as late as 1982 – Clint Eastwood's *Honkytonk Man*.

Character actor Richard Jaeckel played the volatile son of one of the local town's leading citizens. The boyish Jaeckel has appeared in many films in supporting roles and was nominated for an Academy Award for his performance in

Paul Newman's *Sometimes a Great Notion* (UK title: *Never Give an Inch*) in 1971.

Rodd Redwing, who was a true Indian, appeared as a brave in the film and off-set he instructed Elvis in the art of gunplay, something at which he was greatly adept. He also featured eight years later in Elvis's last western *Charro!*

In the story Elvis is cast as Pacer, youngest son of Neddy (Dolores del Rio) and Sam Burton (John McIntire). With older half-brother Clint (Steve Forrest) the family painstakingly work their sprawling ranch on the plains of Texas. A band of renegade Kiowa Indians attack a neighbouring ranch which they completely destroy; the family is wiped out, except for one badly wounded survivor. The insurgent

47

Indians, led by Buffalo Horn (Rudolph Acosta) visit the Burton ranch to find out if they are allies or enemies. Neddy is a full-blooded Kiowa and Pacer is a half-breed. Only Sam and Clint are real white people.

Pacer informs the warriors that the family's considerations are strictly integral – they are a family unit and have no quarrel with Indians or whites. The townspeople view the situation differently. Pacer is feared and despised by most of them because of his Indian blood. Even Clint gains little respect from his contemporaries because of his family position.

The Burtons are unwillingly drawn into the troubles when some of their cattle are scattered and slain. During this time Neddy is assaulted by two wandering trappers. Pacer reacts by violently beating them both almost to death. He and his mother then visit the Kiowa camp only to find that Neddy is now shunned by her own people because she married a white man. Pacer attempts to comfort her, but on their journey home she is shot by the now deranged survivor of the ranch attack. In his wounded state he had been wandering among the hills. Reacting swiftly, Pacer kills him, thinking he is just another marauder.

Clint and Pacer ride to the crossing in the hope that the doctor will attend their seriously wounded mother. He is dissuaded from doing so by everyone, and thus, in desperation, the brothers force him at gunpoint to accompany them. When they return to the ranch they discover that Neddy has in fact died. She had informed Sam that she had seen the Flaming Star of Death just before she passed away.

After her burial, the distraught Pacer blaming everyone at the crossing for her death because they delayed the assistance which might have saved her, seeks vengeance and his immediate target is the doctor. Clint and Pacer have a violent exchange after which the latter leaves to join the Kiowas. In his grief and without his beloved mother he now sees them as 'his people'.

Shortly after his departure his father is attacked and killed by a band of young Indian warriors on their way to meet

48

Buffalo Horn. Clint discovers his body and after burying him beside Neddy, sets off on the trail of the Kiowas with a grim determination – to seek out and kill Buffalo Horn.

Clint accomplishes this mission but is badly wounded in the process. Pacer rescues him from further harm and with the Kiowas now realizing his allegiance to his white brother, they hunt him down. Having seen his injured brother safely to the crossing Pacer now faces a fierce duel with the embittered Indians.

The following day Clint awakens at the crossing to be informed that a rider is approaching. It is Pacer, who is only hours away from death. He simply wants to see if his brother is safe. In an impassioned plea he asks Clint to live on for him because people could never understand a man like him. His last wish is to die in the hills as he has witnessed the Flaming Star of Death. Clint looks on helplessly as Pacer rides away.

The minimal amount of music in the film was quickly dispensed with. Apart from the title song in the credits, Elvis sang 'A Cane and a High Starched Collar' at the opening party. From that point on there were no more songs. Though Elvis and Don Siegel wanted no songs whatsoever, the studio had other ideas. Four songs were actually recorded for the soundtrack, so the inclusion of two of these was a compromise.

Elvis Presley's performance in *Flaming Star* was magnificent. The fact that he had acted superbly was echoed by everyone connected with the film. Writer Clair Huffaker said, 'Elvis Presley has accomplished in this picture what Frank Sinatra accomplished in *From Here to Eternity* – become recognized as a serious, capable actor.' Sinatra had won an Oscar for his role as Private Maggio in Fred Zinnemann's 1953 war classic. In comparison, Elvis's performance in *Flaming Star* was far stronger and emotional. Although there have been Oscar winning actors in the western genre (*High Noon*, *The Big Country* and *True Grit* for example), it was an area generally overlooked by the Academy. More to the point, nobody, it seemed, would want to nominate Elvis Presley for a film award. This was a cruel fact, and Elvis's

shining hour on screen duly went unrecognized by the Film Academy. His performance in the film was quite conceivably the best ever by a singer in a dramatic role.

Don Siegel felt that he had elicited a tremendous feat of acting from Elvis once he had made him aware of what he expected. He said:

> I found him to be very sensitive and actually quite good, with the limitation that he was rather insecure of himself – very insecure. Apparently he believed that he could do better, even though his advisors, especially the Colonel, were definitely against him being cast in such a role. They would have preferred it if he sang throughout the whole movie. They obviously did not want him to dismount from his winning horse, which was just headed for profit-making and nothing else. However, once I got him to relax, I was able to bring out excellent acting abilities in him, in my opinion.
>
> I always had problems getting through to him, when I wasn't alone with him. Those were rare and precious moments, since he avoided being alone with anyone. He always needed to have his people around him for moral support. I wasn't very interested in working with Elvis any more after this film beause he was, well, so distanced.

In the 1972 radio broadcast 'The Elvis Presley Story', which was in twelve one-hour parts, Don Siegel commented that Elvis was seen as something of a laughing stock within the Hollywood film industry – as a direct result of the material he was accepting. It must have been a great disappointment for Siegel to see Elvis stagnate as an actor after his magnificence in *Flaming Star*.

Elvis listens intently to director Don Siegel. Siegel is renowned for his excellent screen career and was undoubtedly the best director Elvis ever worked with. Regrettably, this was to be their only collaboration.
FLAMING STAR

Siegel recalled an amusing incident when he guested on the 'Cinema' television programme in May 1973. This edition was devoted to his films, and he mentioned that in 1962, when he reported for work on *Hell is for Heroes*, the star of that film, Steve McQueen, was extremely wary of him because a rumour had circulated around Hollywood that Elvis Presley had taught Don Siegel the finer points of karate on the set of *Flaming Star* two years earlier.

The studio's decision to include two of the four intended songs brought this later comment from Siegel: 'I think the studio made a mistake. They should have put on a campaign emphasizing that Elvis emerged as an actor in the film. If they were not going to sell it properly, they shouldn't have released it.'

On the set of *Kid Galahad* in late 1961, Elvis himself commented on the studio's intransigence regarding the music for *Flaming Star* to Albert Hand (founder of *Elvis Monthly*):

You know, they do some queer things with soundtracks, cutting things and putting things in. Take the picture *Flaming Star* for instance. Now when that movie was made, there were four songs in it. I considered they should all go out. I considered that this was a dramatic role, and I wanted to keep it that way. For days and days I fought, and in the end they did cut out two of them. Do you know, they even had me singing one of them on the back of a horse – 'Breeches' or something! [actually the song was called 'Britches' and was belatedly released on record in 1978] – but that did get cut finally, and also another one. But it still left two, and if I had had my way, there would have been nothing.

Of Elvis's physically demanding scenes and his graceful stealth, co-star Dolores del Rio said, 'He moves like a young panther.'

People within the film industry, although unconnected with *Flaming Star* directly, also made glowing reports. In a 1979 review of the film the eminent British film director, writer and actor Bryan Forbes had this to say:

Superior Elvis Presley film which demonstrates that he had more acting talent than many critics gave him credit for. It is so fashionable to knock success these days and as a nation we would rather gloat over failure. Elvis spawned many inferior imitations, but he was possessed of extraordinary charisma, projecting a sullen, brooding talent that, like James Dean, captured the imagination of a whole generation. People need causes and the young need gods. In this example of art, for art it was, he plays a half-breed Indian forced to choose between family loyalties when his mother's tribe go on the warpath. It is generally acknowledged to be his best film.

What finer praise could the film have received than this? In a personal communication with Bryan Forbes he commented to me thus: 'Had I had the opportunity, I would have loved to have worked with Elvis Presley, because I think he did have, at the height of his powers, a quite unique talent, both as a singer and as a screen personality.'

Elvis's mother Gladys was descended from the Cherokee tribe, so portraying an Indian was not as alien to Elvis as one might have thought. In December 1960, Elvis was inducted into the Los Angeles Indian Tribal Council by Chief Wah-Nee-Ota, in recognition of his 'constructive portrayal of a man of Indian blood'. On the other hand, *Flaming Star* was banned in South Africa beause of its plot of warring races.

Delmer Daves's 1950 western *Broken Arrow* was considered to be the first film to give a sympathetic slant to the American Indian. *Flaming Star* very much reinforced this issue. Before and between these two films, and indeed up until Ralph Nelson's *Soldier Blue* and Arthur Penn's *Little Big Man* (both 1970), almost all westerns depicted Indians as nothing more than savage miscreants. Accurate accounts of life in the American West in the late nineteenth century tell a vastly different story. Hollywood's Old West was a mythical land, filled with errant heroes and equally dedicated 'bad guys'; but the true picture does not make for solidly entertaining, successful cinema.

Playing an outcast, a loner, seemed perfectly suited to Elvis. The plot gives early indications of the character's outcome. It is painfully inevitable that Pacer has to die – he simply belongs nowhere. He is a man devoid of feeling, except for his own family, to whom he is fiercely loyal.

The final, poignant scene with his father is filled with great sadness. They both realize that they will never see each other again. As they embrace for the very last time, his father profoundly says: 'I guess folks ain't never been fair with you, Pacer. They take a man for what they think he ought to be –

not for what he is.'

These eloquent lines could almost have been applied to Elvis himself in later life. He was never allowed to be just an ordinary man. His overpowering image transcended the stark realities of life, and he himself found this a difficult burden to carry.

The haunting *Flaming Star* was a moment of brilliance in Elvis Presley's questionable film career. He was charged with an innate fury that unleashed itself to such a degree that the screen became a magnetic focus – a disturbing image of enforced racial restraint. The anxiety within his characterization strongly reflected contemporary social issues. Dominating the film's atmosphere was the protagonist's quandary over which race to sympathize with, and his various moral dilemmas were powerfully captured.

It is extremely unlikely, but if ever a posthumous award was to be granted to Elvis Presley for his contribution to films, then *Flaming Star* should leap to the front of any reappraisal. It was and *is* a thought-provoking cinematic experience. RIP Pacer Burton a.k.a. Elvis Presley.

Wild in the Country

Wild in the Country, which began filming in November 1960, marked yet another significant departure for Elvis in that it was a far more literary subject than just about every other script that he accepted.

Based on the novel *The Lost Country* by J.R. Salamanca, the screenplay was written by the much-acclaimed playwright and screenwriter Clifford Odets, who had previously co-written, amongst other things, the classic 1957 movie *Sweet Smell of Success*. The then prestigious Jerry Wald was appointed as producer, and the directional reins were given to Philip Dunne.

The cast, consisting of players like Hope Lange, John Ireland, Tuesday Weld and Millie Perkins gave support in roles which had strong characterization and real significance, unlike many future films. In such stalwart company Elvis responded admirably. As the wayward Glenn Tyler, he convincingly brought to the screen a sensitive portrayal of the misunderstood young man – a subject not altogether unfamiliar in the cinema. In the previous decade James Dean had excelled in this particular genre.

In the story Elvis is Glenn Tyler, youngest of two sons (elder brother Hank is played by Elvis's long-time friend Bobby 'Red' West). After a vicious fight between the two, Glenn is put on a charge, and the court decides that he is to be placed on probation.

He has to report to a psychiatric consultant (Hope Lange) each week and following his initial stormy meeting with her, he becomes attracted to her. Glenn's own girlfriend (Millie Perkins) tries to keep him out of trouble and he also becomes an emotional target for his teenage cousin (Tuesday Weld) when he goes to work for his uncle (William Mims).

An affluent lawyer (John Ireland) also has designs on the consultant and his scheming son (Gary Lockwood) is a sworn enemy of Glenn's, following an incident involving an allegedly stolen car.

55

The psychiatrist sees in Glenn a talent as a writer although he stubbornly resists her encouragement. Eventually she persuades him to write and is so impressed with his work that she arranges to see a university professor in order to ascertain whether or not Glenn would be eligible for a scholarship.

Glenn's naturally truculent personality leads him off the straight path and his attraction for his benefactor is not readily reciprocated. After another incident with the lawyer's son, Glenn accidentally kills him, not realizing that he has a weak heart.

In an attempt to vindicate Glenn in court the psychiatrist is unsuccessful. Harbouring great feelings of guilt following her courtroom failure and fully aware of her strong feelings for Glenn, which she now cannot express, she returns home and tries to commit suicide. The lawyer informs the court of the true nature of his son's health; Glenn is set free, then immediately rushes to comfort the recovering consultant.

She later accompanies him to the train station, where he is about to set off to achieve that unfulfilled ambition – a scholarship.

The music in the film consists of only a few songs and despite the strong dramatic atmosphere, they fit in considerably well. Two songs recorded for the film, 'Lonely Man' and 'Forget Me Never', were cut from the final print. The title song was released as a single and in September 1961 reached number two in the charts.

Hope Lange, as the social worker assigned to bring about Elvis's reform, became the focus of the 'older woman' romance in the plot, and played very well against Elvis's rebellious character. Miss Lange had appeared in producer Jerry Wald's 1957 film *Peyton Place* and was nominated for an Academy Award for her performance. In the 1961 film *Return to Peyton Place*, again produced by Jerry Wald, Tuesday Weld appeared. Both these films, like *Wild in the Country*, were made by 20th Century Fox.

It was a revelation to see Elvis in a role with some depth, playing a man possessed with a latent talent for writing. There are several scenes when Elvis's acting is simply

A dramatic performance by Elvis as a non-conformist on probation for acts of violence. This type of part was clearly Elvis's true *métier* as a screen actor, but was soon to be dismissed in favour of lightweight musicals. His co-star on this occasion was Tuesday Weld. WILD IN THE COUNTRY

outstanding, particularly when he is describing what he views as the injustices in his life. Whilst he is being vouched for in the early courtroom scene, in an attempt to show the inherent goodness in him, he is asked to quote and translate the Master's cry from the cross. ('Eli, Eli, lama sabachthani?' or 'My God, my God, why hast Thou forsaken me?') This he does unhesitatingly and also states just where it can be found

57

in the Bible (Matthew 27:46). His expressions at that point are indeed memorable.

In his initial meeting with the psychiatrist at her home, he touchingly describes the depressing life his mother has endured and explains poetically of what he has dreamed for her. She died when he was eight years old, thus depriving him of any opportunity to change her oppressed existence. Having experienced the death of his own beloved mother Gladys just two years prior to making this film, Elvis's poignant words in the script seemed very appropriate to his own life and in conveying his helplessness, I am sure that personal events were evoked during this portrayal.

Conversely, amidst all this tender emotion there were frequent outbursts of violence from Elvis's character, both

A tender scene with Millie Perkins. The once hostile man leaves for college to pursue a career in writing.

WILD IN THE COUNTRY

verbal and physical. His own explanation of this barely controllable hostility was highly descriptive: 'It's like I'm always walking around with a full cup of anger, trying not to spill it. When somebody hurts me I can't help it, I want to hurt them right back.' The feel of post-adolescent *Angst* within this performance seemed perfectly suited to Elvis, and had the public accepted his dramatic tendencies then, we might never have seen him in another musical film at all. Even as early in his film career as 1960, Elvis himself had hoped to appear in non-singing roles and it is likely that he would have been far happier had this been the situation. The sad fact is that at the close of his screen career, after thirty-three films, he only made one, *Charro*! in 1968, in which he did not sing at all (the title song was heard over the credits, but Elvis was not seen singing).

The sheer emotional drama that was the essence of *Wild in the Country* ironically proved to be greatly responsible for the film's comparative failure at the box-office. This was a rather sad indictment of the taste of film-goers. The handling of the promotion for the film was ill-conceived. On both the US and British advertising bills we had a smiling Elvis, guitar in hand, and the words, 'Elvis Presley sings of love to Hope Lange, Tuesday Weld, Millie Perkins.' To see this, and then to view the film, was like comparing two entirely different issues. The marketing was, in fact, a total absurdity and highly detrimental to the intended impact of the film.

After putting Elvis in three dramatic roles, 20th Century Fox must have seen something in him other than a star of light-hearted musical romps. Alas, this avenue was not followed until the late 1960s, by which time, Elvis had all but lost interest and was too excited about a) his TV special, and b) his impending return to the stage after eight years.

Wild in the Country was screened as part of a late-night Elvis Presley film season at the Glasgow Film Theatre in 1975. At that time, I had communication, both personally and in correspondence with the then administrator Martyn Auty regarding the Elvis canon. Mr Auty is a film critic for the British Film Institute's *Monthly Film Bulletin* and he was also a contributor to the volumes of *The Movie* published in the early 1980s. He commented to me then that he felt that *Wild in the Country* was a film which was 'misunderstood by most people'. Perhaps he was right.

Sadly, with the completion of *Wild in the Country*, that which was Elvis's true *métier* as a cinema artiste – the 'angry young man' – was effectively quelled forever.

Blue Hawaii

In March of 1961, Elvis and his entourage travelled to Hawaii to perform a concert at the Bloch Arena, Pearl Harbor, to benefit the USS *Arizona* Memorial Fund. The Battleship USS *Arizona* had been sunk by the Japanese with the loss of many hundreds of lives in the first attack on America in December 1941, thereby initiating US entry into World War II.

After the concert, Elvis stayed on in Hawaii to make what turned out to be his most lavish and successful film.

Blue Hawaii was directed by Norman Taurog and produced by Hal Wallis. The screenplay was written by Hal Kanter from a story by Allan Weiss.

The co-stars included Joan Blackman (in the first of her two films with Elvis) as the leading female attraction. Angela Lansbury, in a nicely caricatured 'southern mama' performance, played Elvis's mother with whom he is in constant conflict. Miss Lansbury has had a long and distinguished career in films and on stage. She was nominated for an Academy Award for her role in George Cukor's *Gaslight* (1944), her very first film.

In the story Elvis is cast as Chad Gates, a happy-go-lucky beach boy. Much to the chagrin of his wealthy parents he is totally uninterested in being part of the successful family-run pineapple business. He is more content spending time with friends who are considered by his class-conscious parents as undesirable.

In a fit of individualism Chad becomes employed as a tourist guide, thus bringing him into contact with a party of schoolgirls and their attractive teacher. As a result, Chad's Hawaiian girlfriend Maile (Joan Blackman) becomes increasingly jealous. Chad is involved in a fight with a boisterous tourist and is promptly sacked after spending a night in jail.

Under his own authority Chad continues the girls' tour and they set off for Kauai. Maile arrives to find him in what she thinks is a compromising situation. Between her fury and his futile explanations the problem is only exacerbated, but finally she accepts his innocence and the story ends with their lavish wedding ceremony.

The film opens with Elvis having just returned from his army service (several later films would also open this way). The most notable fact about this occasion was that he was supposed to be returning from two years' service in Europe. This again parallelled his own life, and, moreover, the film seemed very much like a sequel to *GI Blues* – a kind of 'Tulsa goes to Hawaii' picture. When both films were coupled in a 1974 re-release by Grand National Pictures (who gained distribution rights from Paramount for these and other Presley films), the sequel idea seemed even more obvious.

Continuing on this theme, in an era (the 1960s) when film sequels were not particularly common (with the exception perhaps of the phenomenally successful James Bond series), Elvis's films were invariably conceived as 'one off' projects, and follow-ups would have created problems. In quite a number of his films, he ends up happily paired off with the leading lady, leaving no real logical extension for the story. Only with Elvis's final, post-1967 film work could we see the possibility of character continuation. More could have been heard, for instance, from the irresponsible Joe Lightcloud of *Stay Away, Joe* in yet another wayward adventure. What became of gunfighter Jess Wade of *Charro!* could have been moulded into another interesting western tale. Lastly, Dr John Carpenter from Elvis's final scripted film *Change of Habit* could have gone on from his work as a ghetto doctor into a big-city hospital situation, perhaps. This is all simply food for thought – in today's cinema the sequel is very much in vogue.

Blue Hawaii affirmed quite definitely, the foundation that had been laid with *GI Blues*. Place Elvis in a location with nice scenery; surround him with young, lively co-stars; throw in a good measure of songs, the odd fight and *voilà* – the blend is perfect. It is easy to see why the maxim of 'Don't knock a successful formula' was not tampered with, but regarding artistic fulfilment many questions could be asked.

The visual splendour of *Blue Hawaii*, particularly the scenes on Kauai, clearly showed that the film had taken considerable time and finance to produce. There were fourteen songs on the soundtrack, more than any other film before or after (except for the two MGM documentaries). One other song, 'Steppin' out of Line' was cut from the final print, and later turned up on Elvis's (non-film) *Pot Luck with Elvis* LP. A song called 'Playing with Fire' is rumoured to have been recorded for the soundtrack, but nothing has ever been heard of it. The soundtrack was, collectively, very good indeed. More care seemed to be taken with the choice of material, and this proved to work for RCA, because it was Elvis's best-selling album ever, for which he received not one, but two Gold Awards. This was a considerable achievement for a soundtrack album in 1961. Remember, this was long before the days of *Saturday Night Fever* and *Grease* type mega-promotion. In February 1962 Elvis again attained the coveted number one spot in the singles chart with the film's 'Rock-A-Hula Baby'/'Can't Help Falling in Love', gaining a singles Gold Award this time.

Everything connected with the film seemed just right. Elvis himself looked very happy and comfortable on screen. Perhaps he did not see this as a definite pattern-former and thought he could easily switch back to a serious role. It was to be seven years and twenty films later before he returned to a fully-fledged dramatic part.

Angela Lansbury, an actress of considerable success before and after *Blue Hawaii*, stated in an interview in the early 1980s that her family had attempted to dissuade her from appearing in the film. This was partly due to the fact that she was only ten years older than Elvis; but I fear that this advice was more typical of the Hollywood stigma which, sadly, was associated with Elvis Presley films. I recall in *Photoplay* film magazine in late 1964 when *Roustabout* was released, that the reviewer could only state: 'What on earth is Barbara Stanwyck doing in an Elvis Presley film?' It was almost as if he alone was some rare form of terminal cinematic disease. This was a very unhealthy attitude to Elvis; it was unfair and caused incalculable damage to his credibility as an actor. He never stated it publicly, but deep down he was very resentful of this attitude and no doubt this was greatly responsible for his disillusionment with the film industry as a whole.

Blue Hawaii introduced us to Howard McNear, who played the boss of the tour company, at times having to be reminded that Elvis in fact worked for him. This forgetful character proved a refreshingly funny foil, and Howard McNear was to repeat a similar characterization in two further Elvis films, namely *Follow That Dream* and *Fun in Acapulco*.

Character actor Steve Brodie appeared in *Blue Hawaii* as a troublesome tourist, and he too was to repeat this role three years later in *Roustabout*. On both occasions, he was involved in a fist fight with Elvis.

Joan Blackman was a competent leading lady, and returned two films later as Elvis's romantic interest in *Kid Galahad*. In Las Vegas in the 1970s Elvis joked to the audience about the 'Hawaiian Wedding Song' marriage sequence, saying that 'It seemed so real I thought I really married the chick!'

With rare exceptions, the big hit song from the film, 'Can't Help Falling in Love', was Elvis's closing song (always dedicated to the audience) from his return to the stage in July 1969 until his final concert in Indianapolis on 26 June 1977. He had obviously considered the song a great personal favourite

When Elvis spoke of his film career during his Las Vegas concerts, he almost always mentioned *Blue Hawaii*, although usually in a cursory fashion. By that time of course he was very much into self-deprecatory remarks about his movies, declaring very few of them as memorable.

Blue Hawaii remains Elvis's most successful film ever. In 1961, no doubt, the script did look right for him. It is a sad irony that this same success led to his eventual fall from grace within the industry. Critics simply saw every new film as a copy and an inferior one at that. There is perhaps some basis for agreement with this, but Elvis was not alone in sticking to a formula that worked. In how many light-hearted 'good ol' boy' films did Burt Reynolds appear, for instance?

A fun-filled musical romp. Elvis and co-star Joan Blackman become romantically entangled in the warm waters of Hawaii. Elvis was to film there again on two further occasions.
BLUE HAWAII

I have lost count. It is pointless to criticize this because many performers will stay with a successful system once it has been established. For example, making a great many westerns over the years did not exactly damage John Wayne's career to any extent.

Shooting *Blue Hawaii* marked the beginning of a love-affair between Elvis and the fiftieth state. He spent many holidays there, made two more feature films there, and gave his Kui Lee Cancer Drive concert – the historic 'Aloha from Hawaii via Satellite' – in January 1973, from the Honolulu International Center.

In retrospect the decision to make *Blue Hawaii was* the right one. Somewhere along the line, possibly in mid-production, or more likely after its enormous success, someone settled on the idea that future Elvis Presley films should follow a similar format. *That* was undoubtedly the wrong decision and a very costly one at that.

Follow That Dream

Before the true formula cycle (if that is what it can be termed) really took off, Elvis made two films in succession for the Mirisch Corporation at United Artists, beginning with *Follow That Dream*. This was filmed in Florida during the summer of 1961.

The director was Gordon Douglas, who has made some films with Frank Sinatra, including *The Detective* (1968), *Tony Rome* (1967) and the sequel to the latter, *Lady in Cement* (1968). Appointed as producer was David Weisbart, who was thereby credited with the production of exactly one third of Elvis's cinematic output to that date.

Follow That Dream was based on the novel *Pioneer Go Home* by Richard Powell. Written in 1957, the novel had the distinction of being published in abridged form in the *Reader's Digest*. The extremely sharp screenplay was written by Charles Lederer, who had written or co-written a substantial number of successful films including Henry Hathaway's *Kiss of Death* (1947), Howard Hawks's *The Thing from Another World* (1951), and *Gentlemen Prefer Blondes* (1953) for Hawks again.

Elvis was here playing a well-meaning but hopelessly naive country boy, and his co-stars supported him admirably. Veteran actor Arthur O'Connell was quite superb as the crafty Pop Kwimper. Anne Helm was the female interest, alongside Joanna Moore who played a scheming welfare officer. Simon Oakland and Jack Kruschen performed well as the would-be mobsters.

In this unusual story, Elvis is Toby Kwimper, who along with his family are homesteading on public property, more by accident (since their vehicle has run out of gasolene on that particular piece of land) than by design. The group consists of Toby, his father, a teenage girl and a trio of very young children, who are distantly related to the Kwimpers. This indeterminate relationship in fact raises custodial problems later. Due to the brusque and authoritarian manner with which they are ordered to vacate the area, the immensely stubborn Pop Kwimper declares war on those in control. This basis provides a very neat set-piece for a whole series of escapades concerning their plight.

Into this territorial mêlée come further homesteaders and a huge caravan which is in fact a 'mobile nightclub' operated by two high-living criminals. Following complaints about behaviour at the nightclub, Toby reluctantly accepts the appointment of surrogate sheriff. In this capacity he informs the lawbreakers that they will have to mend their ways drastically. The infuriated pair make two attempts to dispose of Toby – both unsuccessful.

A legal battle over custody of the children ensues, and only through their simple honesty do they win their case. Everyone is content, and Toby looks upon life, and girls, with a new meaning.

Elvis's performance in the film indicated that perhaps there was a place for him in well-written comedy. His comic flair was a revelation, his bewildered expressions engaging. This vehicle was an excellent change of direction for Elvis and sadly, the quality of the comedy was never quite matched in any future film.

Throughout the film there are frequent references to Toby's lack of education and how unfortunate it is for him to be hindered in this way. This almost suggests that it was conceived more as a tear-jerker than a comedy, but his educational shortcomings are treated in such a humorous fashion that hardly for one moment do we sympathize with him.

Open questions about adult relationships are raised, for example when Toby asks the teenage Holly (Anne Helm): 'Do you know anything about sex?' She awkwardly replies in the affirmative and displays much annoyance when he questions her frequently on the subject. There is a lovely scene in the bank when, in a simple effort to establish who is related to whom, Toby is asked if Holly is his wife. In his innocent way he answers: 'No sir, she just lives with me.' The awkward pause in the air following this reply (for everyone but Toby) was highly effective. Holly did indeed live with Toby and his

Elvis relaxes quietly while co-star Anne Helm studies the script. The novel on her lap is Richard Powell's *Pioneer Go Home*, on which the film was based.
FOLLOW THAT DREAM

father, but more like a family member, rather than in a state of concubinage. There is also a clever running joke about Toby learning the multiplication tables and he explains how he also employs this to curb any sexual desires that he might have.

In the construction of the story, we can perhaps see leftist tendencies of the screenwriter, as the theme is very definitely anti-government, though dealt with in a light-hearted way.

69

The only serious part of the film is the courtroom scene, where the Kwimpers' rights as guardians for three young children are under threat. Elvis excels in this scene, with an extremely emotional defence speech. Relating the honesty and inherent goodness of his father in a very simple way, he concludes by challenging: 'If you don't know that, you ain't no judge!'

A superb comedy with a surprisingly adept performance by Elvis. His sudden transition from drama to musicals and comedy was a revelation and showed that Elvis could diversify.
FOLLOW THAT DREAM

The music in the film was extremely pleasant, consisting of a mere five songs and a four-track EP was released from the soundtrack. The fifth song, 'Sound Advice', was released three years later on the (non-film) *Elvis for Everyone* album.

Follow That Dream received good reviews upon release, with some critics considering that comedy was indeed a suitable area for Elvis. It was perhaps surprising just how smoothly he had made the transition from straight drama and musical production into comedy. It was also very unfortunate that he was never given another script with equal comic content. Once again, Elvis appeared very comfortable in the role he played, and of all the films he was later to criticize, I would imagine that he was not including *Follow That Dream* among them.

The film was a sterling effort to present Elvis in a *different* way and still satisfyingly entertain an audience. It remains his funniest film.

Kid Galahad

In late 1961, Elvis began shooting *Kid Galahad* on location at Idyllwild, California. This was his second film for United Artists and his tenth feature film.

David Weisbart produced for the fourth and final time on an Elvis Presley film. The director was Phil Karlson, who, although not as widely acclaimed as a Ford, or a Wellman, had directed several engrossing smaller-budget crime thrillers, mostly in the 1950s. Included among these are *Tight Spot* (1955) with Edward G. Robinson, *The Phenix City Story* (1955) and *The Scarface Mob* (1959). The screenplay was written by William Fay, based on the 1936 novel by Francis Wallace.

The story had first been filmed by Warner Brothers in 1937. Wayne Morris had played the title role in that version, and the main stars were Edward G. Robinson and Bette Davis. Coincidentally, the director of this first effort was Michael Curtiz, who was to work with Elvis twenty-one years later on *King Creole*.

In 1941, Warners remade the film as *The Wagons Roll at Night*, with a different slant on the storyline. The common link in these two earlier films was the appearance of Humphrey Bogart.

What is perhaps most surprising about a novel that was transferred to the screen on three occasions, is that it was a rather dull book, full of typical gangster story clichés. Its attraction as a cinema property had more to do with the basic theme, than the overall content.

In this final version, Elvis was given the clumsy name of Walter Gulick. The only thing retained here from the novel was the initials, as in the book the 'Kid' was known as Ward Gruisenberry, if anything an even clumsier name.

The cover of the novel proclaimed the story thus: 'Gamblers, Girls and a Soft-hearted Kid with the Killer Instinct.' Likewise, this applied as a fair description of the film. Elvis's keen interest in athletics, football and especially karate, helped to get him in shape for what was undoubtedly his most physically demanding role. Mushy Callahan, an ex-fighter and experienced trainer, was appointed as boxing advisor on the set, and he was to make glowing comments on Elvis's response to coaching.

The co-stars were of a decidedly higher calibre than many other productions. Gig Young played the troubled owner of the training camp. He was a very accomplished actor who began his professional career under his own name, Byron Barr, but changed it to Gig Young after playing a character of that name in an early film called *The Gay Sisters* in 1942. He was the recipient of an Academy Award for his performance in Sydney Pollack's *They Shoot Horses, Don't They?* in 1969. Gig Young died in 1978 under tragic circumstances in a shooting incident.

Charles Bronson played the weary, laconic trainer in the story. It seems that he and Elvis were fairly distanced on the film set. Bronson was apparently unimpressed with Elvis's stature as a performer. In a biography of Bronson by David Downing, the star had this to say about his participation: 'My wife and I went to see the film, and it was so bad we left the theatre in a hurry while it was still running.' At the time of *Kid Galahad* he was a supporting actor, but later went on to international stardom. Bronson's screen career has itself been inconsistent, which makes his criticism of other performers all the more surprising.

The leading female roles were taken by Lola Albright, and Joan Blackman in her second and last film with Elvis.

The story opens with Elvis, as Walter Gulick, fresh out of the army and broke. Of this predicament he shyly quips: 'I got in a crap game with my separation pay, and it got separated from me.' More by accident than intention, and by way of earning a fast five dollars a round, he accepts an offer to spar with an up-and-coming young fighter. In the first round, and with his first blow, he lays the young prospect out cold. Willy Grogan (Gig Young), the enterprising but penniless promoter who runs the camp, sees an opportunity to solve all his financial problems and assigns his

73

Above: Elvis takes instruction from former prize-fighter Mushy Callahan who coached, among others, Errol Flynn. Callahan appeared in the film as a referee. *Right*: Elvis's long-time friend Red West once commented about 'always ending up on my ass' in fight scenes, and it's about to happen again. Elvis's background in football and karate ensured his fitness for such a demanding role.

KID GALAHAD

worldly-wise trainer Lew Nyack (Charles Bronson) to make a proper fighter out of him.

Walter meets and falls for Willy's sister Rose Grogan (Joan Blackman) but incurs the disapproval of Willy in the process. Meanwhile, Dolly Fletcher (Lola Albright), who is Willy's 'fiancée', is trying to make an emotionally charged decision about whether to leave him or not.

Following a heated private fight, Walter is dubbed 'Kid Galahad', and that becomes his fighting name. He wins bout after bout, and plans to open a garage after he has made enough money from boxing. Willy is outraged when Walter and Rose announce their plan to marry. In his last climactic fight, which criminals attempt to rig, the Kid wins, and his long-term plans can now be realized.

The fight scenes, like boxing films before (*Body and Soul*, *Champion*) and after (the *Rocky* series, *Raging Bull*), were brutal and painfully convincing. In the final bout, the Kid's opponent was Ramon 'Sugar Boy' Romero, who was in fact one Ramon de la Fuente – a *real* boxer and not an actor. This exercise was no doubt intended to lend some realism to the fight, and it succeeded, as this was the most bloody bout in the entire film.

The music consisted of six songs which were all included on an EP of the soundtrack. Like Elvis's previous film, the songs were good, but secondary to the action. The film could easily have stood on its own merits, with no songs whatsoever, as a straight drama. There were enough moments to substantiate this, particularly in one vociferous exchange between Elvis and Gig Young.

The overall presentation had to be admired, and on a relative scale *Kid Galahad* would rank comfortably in the top six of Elvis Presley's films.

This was to be the last film for six full years that would be based on an original novel. Elvis's next sixteen films in succession were all written directly as screenplays – and all were constructed especially for him. This proved over a period of time to be highly detrimental to his career, and not surprisingly it was in this area that most of the severe criticism was made.

3   *The Established Formula (1962–64)*

The problem is, they keep trying to make *GI Blues* and *Blue Hawaii* over and over again, and all they do is move the scenery around a little.

Elvis Presley on film

Girls! Girls! Girls!

The spring of 1962 saw Elvis at work on Paramount's *Girls! Girls! Girls!* with location filming taking place on the Kona coast of Hawaii. Originally, the film was titled *Gumbo Ya Ya* (also *Cumbo Ya Ya*) and was to be set in New Orleans. This odd Creole expression apparently means 'Everybody talks at once', and the significance of this as a title for an Elvis Presley film remains a puzzle. Four years before, the New Orleans-set *King Creole* opened with a pre-credit song called *Gumbo* – a spiritual number sung by black people, and not Elvis. In any event, with an altered title and an entirely different location, the cameras rolled.

Norman Taurog again directed, and on his fifth outing as producer for Elvis, was Hal Wallis. The screenplay was written by Edward Anhalt and Allan Weiss, from a story by the latter. Edward Anhalt, an eminent screenwriter, has two Oscar Awards to his credit – one for *Becket* (1964) and the other for *Panic in the Streets* (1950) – and has written or co-written some notable screenplays including *The Boston Strangler* (1968) and *Jeremiah Johnson* (1972). For some reason, possibly his own, he was not assigned to write another screenplay for Elvis Presley.

77

The female co-stars were the sultry Stella Stevens and one Laurel Goodwin. Stella Stevens is an actress of some considerable merit, and on this occasion she even got to sing three songs herself. Representing the male support was Jeremy Slate (already seen in a brief role in 1960s *GI Blues*) who seemed to be always cast as a heavy. In the role of Sam, the nightclub owner, was Robert Strauss, the excellent character actor who had received a well-deserved Academy Award nomination for his portrayal of 'Animal' in Billy Wilder's much-praised prisoner-of-war drama *Stalag 17* in 1953. Strauss was to appear with Elvis again three years later in *Frankie and Johnny*.

In the story Elvis is Ross Carpenter, the skipper of a fishing boat. When not involved in maritime pursuits, he sometimes sings at a local nightclub. Robin Gantner (Stella Stevens), the resident songstress at the nightclub, and Ross have something of an indefinite relationship. Ross meets Laurel Dodge (Laurel Goodwin), and they begin to see each other more frequently. Meanwhile the *West Wind*, the boat which Ross and his late father lovingly built but which now belongs to someone else, becomes the property of yet another buyer. Ross goes to work for the new owner, Wesley Johnson (Jeremy Slate), in an arrangement whereby he hopes to be able to buy back the boat from him over a period of time. Johnson is an obnoxious employer, and he and Ross are constantly at odds.

Laurel, it transpires, is from a wealthy family, and when she tries to show favour to Ross by purchasing the boat for him, he is appalled and rejects her 'gift'. Ross takes on a singing job as a way of earning more money, and this appointment delights Sam (Robert Strauss), but only serves to infuriate the jealous Robin. After a fight with Johnson, Ross sees the error of his ways regarding Laurel, and is reunited with her. He now plans to build a completely new boat.

Whilst Elvis's performance may not have elevated him to any lofty heights as an actor, he was certainly believable as a man whose first love and sole interest was his boat. Actually the innocuous title was rather misleading, for despite the

The second visit to Hawaii. The titillating title and publicity had little bearing on the story, which concerned fishing and boats more than females.
GIRLS! GIRLS! GIRLS!

presence of the two main female leads, the story had more to do with fishing and boats than with girls. Its commercial viability was far more important to the studio however, so as far as they were concerned why shouldn't it have a catchy, enticing title? This logic succeeded, naturally. The film was a financial hit and Paramount was pleased with the outcome. This success was to continue through a further four films for that studio.

For a great deal of screen time Elvis appeared all in black, including yachting cap. He was extremely fond of this headgear, and many off-set photographs taken over the years show Elvis wearing such a cap.

The soundtrack for *Girls! Girls! Girls!* was excellent. Thirteen songs were incuded on the album, although two of them, 'Where Do You Come From' and 'I Don't Want To' were cut from the final print of the film. In the cinema trailer, Elvis is seen singing part of 'I Don't Want To', and this just adds to the confusion. (This had also happened two years earlier, when Elvis was seen singing the song 'Forget Me Never' in the UK cinema trailer for *Wild in the Country* – the song did not appear in the finished film.)

Having already recorded songs, or at least portions thereof, in languages other than English – 'Wooden Heart' in German for *GI Blues*, and even Polynesian/Hawaiian in 'Aloha Oe' for *Blue Hawaii* we were now treated to hearing Elvis sing in Chinese. Part of the song 'Earth Boy' was sung in true Oriental style by Elvis in a scene with two small Chinese girls.

As with *Blue Hawaii*, an overabundance of songs was recorded, and apart from the two album tracks cut from the film, there were other songs recorded which were shelved completely. These were 'Plantation Rock' (this later emerged on a bootleg album and was then officially released by RCA in 1983), and 'Mama', which *was* featured in the film but not sung by Elvis. His version did not turn up on record until 1970, and then on a budget album. Two more songs were also mentioned at the time, these being 'Twist Me Loose' and 'A Potpourri', but have as yet to make an appearance on vinyl. Elvis also sang part of a song called 'Dainty Little Moonbeams' which is not on record. The exciting 'Return To Sender', taken from the soundtrack, was released as a single, and in December 1962 hit the number one slot, the last song from an Elvis Presley film that would have this distinction.

On the Studio set in Hollywood where they were recording the 'Return to Sender' sequence, Elvis was met by British singing star Billy Fury, there to present Elvis with a record award. Photographs of this meeting then appeared in UK music papers. Shortly after this Billy Fury recorded and released as a single, the song 'Because of Love', which Elvis had sung in *Girls! Girls! Girls!*

It was around this time that the press-named 'Memphis Mafia' (Elvis's coterie of personal friends and bodyguards) began to make noticeable appearances in Elvis's films. Since they were in a sense his 'family', perhaps he could have been accused of a form of nepotism. Most likely he was more at ease having them close at hand. In *Girls! Girls! Girls!* it was Red West who appeared with Elvis playing a boat hand – complete with dyed black hair. West was one of Elvis's

Precocious children were to feature regularly in musical extravaganzas. GIRLS! GIRLS! GIRLS!

earliest friends, having attended Humes High School in Memphis with him, then touring with him on his first singing dates as a kind of general roadie. He had also, at Elvis's request, spent much of Elvis's army service time with him in Germany. Of all the so-called 'Memphis Mafia', he was the most consistent performer in Elvis's films. Prior to *Girls! Girls! Girls!* he was seen in *GI Blues* in a fight scene; had a role as Elvis's bullying brother in *Wild in the Country* in which he even had a few lines of dialogue; could be spotted in a party scene in *Blue Hawaii*; played a bank guard in *Follow That Dream*; and lay stretched out on the canvas as a defeated boxer in *Kid Galahad*. He was to feature in several other Elvis Presley films, and remained part of Elvis's entourage until their unfortunate and bitter parting as friends in 1976, when Red West was sacked along with his cousin Sonny West (also in Elvis's employ for many years) and one Dave Hebler. They sought revenge on Elvis, and with the help of a journalist Steve Dunleavy, published a scathing book *Elvis: What Happened*? which turned up in bookshops in August 1977, the month in which Elvis died.

This suggests that Elvis's choice of friends was somewhat questionable, but that aside, many of these people had a fairly comfortable existence as extras in his films, and several of them remained on amicable terms with him to the end.

Throughout *Girls! Girls! Girls!* Elvis plays his part pretty seriously, with only the odd moment of light relief thrown in. Jeremy Slate, as the hopeful Lothario, is given more of the sharp cynical dialogue. In an exchange with Laurel Goodwin, who clearly detests him, he remarks: 'I know I don't have to push, I know I'm irresistible.'

Whatever Elvis's personal intentions regarding his screen career, at this point his ambitions were stifled. From *Girls! Girls! Girls!* on, Elvis became to all intents and purposes, imprisoned in 'formula' films. This situation is what no doubt gradually led to his artistic enervation.

It Happened at the World's Fair

It Happened at the World's Fair was the title of Elvis's next film, shot in the summer of 1962 for MGM Studios, on location in Seattle.

Norman Taurog stayed on, hot from his previous film with Elvis, as director. The producer this time around was Ted Richmond, and the screenplay was written by Si Rose and Seaman Jacobs.

The film was to be called *Take Me to the Fair* (the title of one of the soundtrack songs) but was changed, in a possible crafty effort to equate it with previous notable films with the 'It Happened' part-title. Frank Capra's glorious 1935 film *It Happened One Night* which had won Oscar Awards for himself as director, and for its two stars, Clark Gable and Claudette Colbert, is undoubtedly one of the most classic film comedies in screen history. In 1947, Frank Sinatra, Jimmy Durante and a cast of musical performers appeared in MGM's *It Happened in Brooklyn*. This effort did not quite match the acclaim of the Capra film, although I should add that this was not necessarily the intention of its makers.

Elvis's co-stars included Gary Lockwood, in his second Presley film (the first being *Wild in the Country*). Joan O'Brien and Yvonne Craig provided the female glamour, while Vicky Tiu, the young Chinese girl to whom Elvis reluctantly becomes guardian is very endearing – easily gaining audience sympathy.

In the story Elvis is cast as Mike Edwards, a bush pilot, who with his close friend Danny Burke (Gary Lockwood) engages in crop-spraying for a living, in their small plane. Due to constant financial problems, their plane is grounded and they are forced to seek work elsewhere. This situation eventually leads them to Seattle, and a chance meeting with Sue-Lin (Vicky Tiu), a precocious Chinese girl. As a result of Danny's gambling, they secure the use of a mobile home. Escorting Sue-Lin to the fair, Mike meets and is attracted to Diane Warren (Joan O'Brien) a nurse at the clinic.

Later, Sue-Lin is taken away by the Child Welfare Board, and Mike is led to believe that Diane was responsible for this action. Danny, meanwhile, has secured a flying job for them, taking freight to Canada. Mike discovers that the freight is illegal furs, and refuses to fly. A fierce fight ensues between Mike and the owner of the goods, and the police arrive to quell the trouble. Sue-Lin comes back under the temporary care of Mike, who now realizes that Diane was innocent of involvement in her removal.

The structure of *It Happened at the World's Fair* suggests something along the lines of a 'buddy' movie – a category of film very popular in the seventies and eighties.

Unlike Elvis's films to date, in which he invariably dressed in very casual clothes, this occasion presented him as a picture of sartorial elegance. In suits specially styled for him by Hollywood's Sy Devore, he looked more like a city businessman than a bush pilot.

Making his screen début was eleven-year-old Kurt Russell who went on to portray Elvis Presley in John Carpenter's woefully inaccurate 1979 'biopic', *Elvis – the Movie*.
IT HAPPENED AT THE WORLD'S FAIR

Vicky Tiu, whose two sisters had featured in Elvis's previous film, proved a very endearing diminutive co-star.
IT HAPPENED AT THE WORLD'S FAIR

The setting, amidst the grandiose surroundings of the World's Fair, was visibly attractive, particularly the breathtaking scenes from the monorail and the famous Space Needle.

The fight scenes in the film, especially the first one (with the now obligatory appearance by Red West) are distinctly brutal for what was essentially a musical production. Action, in the form of fight sequences, was clearly a prerequisite for screenwriters, as precious few of Elvis's films did not include such scenes.

The music, providing enough to fill another soundtrack album was, on the whole, a satisfying blend of ballads mixed with light rock. But this was also an example of songwriters catering just too much for melodies appealing mostly to children. Three songs, 'Take Me to the Fair', 'Cotton Candy Land' and 'How Would You Like to Be' were almost nursery-rhyme in style, and from a total soundtrack of only ten songs, were too much.

'One Broken Heart for Sale', which was a good song, was released as a single from the film, and reached number eight in the charts in March 1963. In the film Elvis sings an extra verse to the song and, as yet, this version has never been officially released by RCA.

A notable fact regarding the film, is that it marked the debut of eleven-year-old Kurt Russell, who would later portray Elvis Presley in a 1978 TV movie of his life. In 1979 it was released in the UK, in a greatly shortened form, as a theatrical film called *Elvis – The Movie*, but even in its 2½-hour complete form, it was a woefully inaccurate affair, and probably should not have been made at all.

It Happened at the World's Fair was, after five years, Elvis's second film for MGM, following *Jailhouse Rock*. The two films could not have been more different. In 1967 they played in a double bill up and down the UK and it was very interesting to note the changes in that relatively short span of time. Cinematically, Elvis the uncaring arrogant slob of 1957, had developed into a humanitarian – courtesy of Metro-Goldwyn-Mayer *et al*.

Fun in Acapulco

In January of 1963 Elvis was working on his next colourful extravaganza for Paramount Pictures, which, like his previous film for that company *Girls! Girls! Girls!*, was produced by Hal Wallis. The director on this occasion was Richard Thorpe, who had worked with Elvis six years earlier on MGM's *Jailhouse Rock*. The screenplay was written by Allan Weiss.

Entitled *Fun in Acapulco*, it involved a crafty piece of trickery played on cinema-goers. The lush scenery, lavish surroundings and Mexican way of life as depicted in the movie, were as alien to Elvis Presley as they were to the viewing audience – because in not one frame of film was he actually in Acapulco. It should have been called *Fun on a Hollywood Film Set*, as all of Elvis's supposed scenes south of the border were either mock-ups or back projection shots. For Mexico, substitute Hollywood, California. That is where Elvis's scenes all took place. Location shots were certainly filmed in Acapulco, with positively the most obvious stand-in anyone is ever likely to have the misfortune to spot. In profile, stature, stance, style of walking and many other features, he looked about as much like Elvis Presley as ET did. Not content with misleading film-goers once, this same professional chicanery was used again, 3½ years later in MGM's *Double Trouble*.

One redeeming factor was the choice of co-stars. Ursula Andress, fresh from her memorable appearance in the original James Bond film, *Doctor No*, was Elvis's leading lady and performed with a certain ebullient flair. The celebrated Hungarian actor Paul Lukas, seen in a few brief scenes, was cast as Miss Andress's discontented father. Lukas had spent many years in films and in 1943 had won an Academy Award for his part in the play-turned-film *Watch on the Rhine*, which was produced by none other than Hal Wallis.

One alleged (though disclaimed) reason for Elvis's non-participation in location scenes was the strong charge

In keeping with the contemporary vogue Elvis performs 'Bossa Nova Baby'.
FUN IN ACAPULCO

that he was in fact *persona non grata* to the Mexican authorities, because he had apparently made a derogatory comment about their natives. Red West later stated that this story was a complete fabrication. Had it been true, then it would seem incongruous to cast Elvis in a film set in a country with which he was in a form of dispute. But the power of the Hollywood film industry can be truly remarkable.

In the story Elvis is Mike Windgren, a trapeze artist, who has come to Mexico from his home state of Florida in order to eradicate the memory of a tragic accident. Shortly after his arrival, he befriends a small, orphaned Mexican boy, Raoul (Larry Domasin), who after hearing Mike sing, insists on becoming his manager. After zealously arranging auditions for Mike at several hotels, Raoul is eventually successful and secures a fairly lucrative contract.

Mike is attracted to Margarita Dauphine (Ursula Andress) and also to a lady bullfighter named Dolores Gomez (Elsa Cardenas). He becomes a lifeguard, much to the chagrin of Moreno (Alejandro Rey), who is the local hero, diving from the high cliffs in a nightly performance.

As a result of the accident that he is trying to forget, Mike now has a morbid fear of heights, but is eventually goaded into attempting to dive from La Quebrada – the highest cliff – himself. He succeeds in this quest, overcoming his acrophobia at the same time. Mike and his Margarita are clearly in love.

A very amusing anecdote from this time is related in the book, *Elvis: What Happened?* Following the spectacular dive Elvis was supposed to have made at the film's climax (courtesy of studio technology), he is joyously hoisted into the air by several appreciative Mexicans, who carry him back to the eagerly waiting Ms Andress. The scene was wasted several times and retakes were necessary due to Elvis moving around too much – the reason allegedly being that one of the men in the group was attempting to interfere with him! Elvis went over to Red West and company and said: 'There's a fag in that bunch. Every time they pick me up, one of them six guys grabs me by the balls.' The offending character was dismissed by the assistant director.

The powerful and visually dramatic 'El Toro'.
FUN IN ACAPULCO

One strangely common fact regarding the storyline, is that in every review found, including those within fan club publications, the information is that Elvis has come to Acapulco to get over an accident in which his 'partner' or 'close friend' (and other descriptions of that ilk) was seriously injured. Towards the end of the film it is made absolutely clear that it was his *brother*, a member of 'The Flying Windgrens' family trapeze act, who was in fact *killed* in said accident. How such a basic fact as this can be misconstrued in various reviews is, quite frankly, beyond comprehension.

The soundtrack music had an appropriately distinctive Latin feel, and was a considerable improvement on the *World's Fair* set. From the lazy title song, through powerfully emotive numbers like 'El Toro' and 'Margarita', to semi-rock with 'Bossa Nova Baby', Elvis's extensive vocal range was well employed. Retaining the multilingual idea on screen, this time Elvis sang a song called 'Guadalajara' completely in Spanish. His rendition was near perfect, with all the correct nuances. 'Bossa Nova Baby' was the obvious choice, with its commercial theme, as a single release, and in November 1963 reached its highest position of number nine.

For a man who began his career in rock and roll, Elvis's transition via films, into other areas of music, could only be admired. He had now involved himself with jazz, Polynesian sounds and Latin rhythm, and seemed more than capable of flowing into any chosen style of music. Of course, the very fact of his amazing versatility fully justified claims of his enormous talent as a singer.

As a tale of one man's emotional vicissitudes, *Fun in Acapulco* stands up reasonably well. The main disappointments with the overall presentation were the fact that Elvis had not visited Mexico at all (a fact that film-goers would of course be unaware of), and the embarrassingly obvious use of stand-ins. But, the box-office receipts were favourable, however, so the studio was not overly concerned with what they probably saw as mere 'minor technicalities'.

Elvis's next film, his fourteenth, would show a marked improvement in quality.

Viva Las Vegas (Love in Las Vegas)

Viva Las Vegas, filmed by MGM, began shooting in the summer of 1963, with an eleven-week work schedule: three weeks on location in Las Vegas, and a further eight weeks back at the Hollywood Studios. Alongside *Blue Hawaii*, this ranks as the most lively, fun-filled vehicle for Elvis Presley, in which he displayed obvious enthusiasm for the project.

The screenplay was written by Sally Benson, and the director (and co-producer) on this occasion was a man long associated with top-class musicals, George Sidney. In the forties, the real heyday of film musicals, he was MGM's most successful director. In that particular era, he directed the Gene Kelly–Frank Sinatra smash *Anchors Aweigh* (1945), and *The Three Musketeers* (1948) with Gene Kelly again. Following this, he then added other notable films to his credit, such as *Annie Get Your Gun* (1950) *Show Boat* (1951), *Kiss Me Kate* (1953) and *Pal Joey* (1957). At that particular time Elvis could not have had a more distinguished or experienced musical director at the helm than George Sidney. The co-producer on the film was Jack Cummings.

The title of the film created some problems for the studio. In 1956 MGM had made a Dan Dailey–Cyd Charisse musical called *Meet Me in Las Vegas* produced by one Joe Pasternak (who would later produce two films for Elvis Presley also at MGM). Upon that film's release in the UK, it was changed to *Viva Las Vegas*! Naturally, to avoid confusion, the title of Elvis's film had to be changed in the UK, and so it became *Love in Las Vegas*. One common link in both films was that the same man, George Stoll, was credited for the music. In fact, for his work in the earlier film, he had received an Academy Award nomination.

Ann-Margret, playing the female lead, undoubtedly proved herself to be Elvis's best co-star ever. She received equal billing (though Elvis's name actually came first) and throughout the film she shone every bit as brightly as Elvis did. A tremendous rapport developed between them which greatly enhanced the film, and their musical sequences together were a delight to behold.

An off-screen romance began at this period, with announcements in the media that they were to be engaged. This sensational news caused domestic problems for Elvis, who had his young Priscilla waiting for him back in Memphis. This relationship seemed to end, however, and Ann-Margret married actor Roger Smith in 1967, the same year that Elvis and Priscilla were wed. Elvis and Ann-Margret remained very close friends, each attending the other's respective Las Vegas performances. She was one of the very few Hollywood people – George Hamilton was another – who attended Elvis's private funeral in Memphis and she was visibly distraught at the loss of such a dear friend.

As an actress, Ann-Margret went on to great heights, and established herself as a dramatic actress of some note. In 1971, she was given an Academy Award nomination for her role in Mike Nichols's *Carnal Knowledge* in which she played opposite Jack Nicholson. She has at times even shunned a glamorous appearance in exchange for a solid film part. She was almost unrecognizable, in a plain-Jane role, in the 1982 UK film *The Return of the Soldier*, playing alongside such stalwart British performers as Alan Bates, Glenda Jackson and Julie Christie. With a tutored English accent, she acquitted herself very well.

Character actor William Demarest played the role of Ann-Margret's father in the film. In a career that began in the late 1930s he played a variety of supporting roles through several decades in the movies. Strangely enough, he appeared with the legendary Al Jolson in *The Jazz Singer* in 1927, and twenty years later would play in the two bio-pics on Jolson's life, with Larry Parks in the title role. Both he and Parks were nominated for an Academy Award for the first instalment *The Jolson Story*.

In the story Elvis is Lucky Jackson, an enthusiastic race driver who arrives in Las Vegas to take part in the prestigious annual Grand Prix. He encounters Rusty Martin (Ann-Margret), as a result of which he is side-tracked from his driving. He finds a formidable rival in Count Elmo Mancini (Cesare Danova), a wealthy Italian racing champion. Lucky and Rusty develop a strong mutual attraction and spend a great deal of time together. Rusty is encouraged in this area by her father (William Demarest), who sees admirable qualities in the young driver.

Lucky has the misfortune (not exactly in keeping with his name) to lose the large amount of money he has set aside for a new engine for his car. He and his devoted mechanic Shorty (Nicky Blair) take jobs as hotel waiters in the meantime.

Both Lucky and Rusty enter a talent contest, which Lucky wins. Disappointingly, he still does not gain the required capital.

With only hours until race time, an engine is delivered (a gesture by Mr Martin) and the ecstatic crew work furiously on its instalment. Lucky enters the race just in time, and is the eventual winner. The story closes with he and Rusty being married.

Viva Las Vegas was the first, and best, of three films in which Elvis would play a racing-car driver. This one had the most excitement, culminating in the climactic race. Elvis, as Lucky Jackson, played a very easy-going type and injected a whole new freshness into his characterization. If, as several reports have informed us, Elvis was bored with his film work by the early 1960s, then he concealed that fact exceptionally well at this time.

The 'Bright Light City' (so named in the title song) of Las Vegas was shown to its fullest, with some dazzling camera work by cinematographer Joseph Biroc, who had, among his credits, worked on the delightful Frank Capra comedy *It's a Wonderful Life* in 1946. Included was a Parisian sequence of the *Folies Bergère* shot with the permission of the Hotel Tropicana.

The soundtrack music was, as expected, plentiful, but a great deal of it remained inexplicably unreleased, or turned up hidden away on some future album. The official release from the film was a mere four-track EP and a single with the title track backed with the Ray Charles song 'What'd I Say'. This single did not fare too well, only achieving the highest

Playing a racing driver on the first of three
occasions. This was by far the most enjoyable.
VIVA LAS VEGAS (LOVE IN LAS VEGAS)

A quiet moment at the piano at which Elvis was highly accomplished. His partnership with the vibrant Ann-Margret proved extremely worthwhile, and their enthusiasm for each other was obvious. They were said to have shared an off-screen romance.
VIVA LAS VEGAS (LOVE IN LAS VEGAS)

chart position of number fifteen in April 1964. Italian was the linguistic choice for what was becoming an obligatory non-English song in each film and this time it was the rather beautiful 'Santa Lucia' which received Elvis's full-voiced treatment.

This song only surfaced in 1965, on the 'Elvis for Everyone' album. Two more songs recorded for, but ultimately cut from, the final film, namely 'Night Life' and 'Do the Vega' did not emerge on record until 1969, and then only on a budget album. Another song recorded for the film, but cut out, 'You're the Boss' has yet to see the light of day. Ann-Margret performed a couple of songs on her own, although one of them, 'My Rival', was cut from the UK version of the film.

Playing guitar on the studio sessions which produced this work at Radio Recorders Studios in Hollywood was none other than Glen Campbell, later to become a recording artist in his own right. Interestingly, his was the last attempt by Hal B. Wallis at film star creation who cast him with John Wayne in *True Grit* and gave him his own starring vehicle in a film called *Norwood*. Unfortunately for Wallis, this optimism did not come to fruition, and Campbell returned to his musical roots.

Meanwhile, the energetic and exciting Elvis Presley that was evidenced in *Viva Las Vegas* was about to take the worst possible step he could have made in his screen career. Under the misguided influence of the overbearing Colonel Parker, he was now entering the arena of economizing on budget. The voracious Colonel decided that they required greater profits, and cared little if there was an obvious decline in quality.

Kissin' Cousins

In October 1963, almost immediately after the completion of his previous MGM movie, Elvis began work on *Kissin' Cousins* for the same studio. The story was set in the Smokey Mountain region of Tennessee, but was actually shot in the mountains outside Los Angeles.

The entire film was completed in a staggering seventeen days. This sudden intensity of time-scale must surely have had Elvis himself wondering what was happening with his film career. Coming straight off a film that had taken almost three months to shoot on to a set that used as little time as that needed to film a television show should have indicated to him that all was not well.

The reason behind this rapid filming schedule was a producer named Sam Katzman. He had been responsible for several 'quickies' in the past, including *Your Cheating Heart* (a bio-pic on Hank Williams), and was obviously seen by Colonel Parker as someone who could successfully expedite Elvis's film projects. He only ever worked on one more Elvis Presley film, but his harmful contribution left a bitter mark on Elvis's screen career.

The director was Gene Nelson, an ex-musical star himself from films like *The Daughter of Rosie O'Grady* (1950). Nelson only ever achieved moderate success in film direction. Like Katzman, he was to work on one more project with Elvis Presley.

The story and screenplay were written by Gerald Drayson Adams (with director Gene Nelson actually co-writing the screenplay), who had written screenplays for several 'costume' films in the early fifties for Universal–International studios. One example of his work was the lightweight *Son of Ali Baba* (1952), starring the then prominent matinee idol, Tony Curtis.

The co-stars were certainly a professional crew. The splendid Arthur O'Connell as the obstinate patriarch, was something of a saving grace in the film, although his

97

performance never quite matched his wonderfully humorous Pop Kwimper from *Follow That Dream*. O'Connell was a reliable character actor for many years and had previously appeared in films as diverse as Orson Welles's classic *Citizen Kane* (1940) and two films with director Joshua Logan in 1956, namely *Bus Stop* and *Picnic*, for which he was nominated for an Academy Award. Arthur O'Connell's performance in *Kissin' Cousins* served to enhance the film, but not quite enough.

In the story Elvis is Lieutenant Josh Morgan of the US Air Force. He is also Jodie Tatum (Morgan's double), an obstreperous hillbilly. As Josh Morgan he is sent by the government to persuade an obdurate rural family to allow a missile base to be built on their land. Having been born and raised in Tennessee himself (an allusion perhaps to Elvis's

Two Elvis Presleys for the price of one was part of the promotional campaign. Despite the idea it was one of the weaker productions, due largely to financial retrenchment.

KISSIN' COUSINS

98

own background), the Lieutenant turns out to be a distant cousin of the family in question. This happy discovery does not preclude monumental problems for the military, before they are reluctantly granted permission. Along the way, Josh makes an enemy of the jealous Jodie and falls for Azalea Tatum (Yvonne Craig). Ma and Pa Tatum (Glenda Farrell and Arthur O'Connell), though initially pleased with the visit by a distant relative, are wary of his motives.

After much wrangling, the persuasive ways of Josh finally win over the Tatums. Happier news still is that Josh and

Clever trick photography did not feature throughout the whole production. The use of stand-ins was embarrassingly obvious.
KISSIN' COUSINS

Azalea are to be married, as are Jodie and Midge (Cynthia Pepper), the Captain's secretary. The family are now delighted with their good fortune.

Someone had the novel idea of presenting Elvis in a dual role, presumably for added effect. The result was simply lukewarm. In a patently obvious blonde wig, Elvis was visibly uncomfortable.

Glenda Farrell, as the philosophical mother, and Jack Albertson as the constantly encumbered captain leading the mountain 'assault', have some agreeably comic moments, but the script never lived up to the standard of earlier films. In fact, some of the dialogue was downright awful, and in one scene, where Elvis was talking on a radio receiver to Jack Albertson about lost soldiers, he uttered, 'Good grief, mine's missing too!' The words 'good grief' are hardly akin to the dialect of a Mississippi native and this just sounded ridiculous. An exclamation like this would be expected more from someone like David Niven or someone else in a 'gentlemanly' role.

The music in the film was written with a deliberately Hillbilly/country feel, and a lot of it is highly effective. In an attempt to obtain this sound the music was recorded, not in Hollywood, but at the RCA studios in Nashville, Tennessee. At least this pointed to a more creative decision.

One song from the album, 'Anyone', was cut from the film, and in another curious twist regarding the music, Glenda Farrell sang a song called 'Pappy' which was not included when the film was released theatrically in the UK, but was reinserted in the 16 mm and TV versions of the film.

There were two completely different songs called 'Kissin' Cousins', one sung over the opening credits, and the other sung at the close of the film. The latter version was released as a single, obviously to promote the film, and coupled with the powerful 'It Hurts Me', climbed to number twelve in the singles charts of July 1964.

The continuity and editing of the film can only be described as cases of gross ineptitude. Lance Le Gault, Elvis's double in the film, did not resemble him in any form, and in his scenes the blonde wig that he wore looked totally different from the one that Elvis sported. In what is surely the greatest *faux pas* in any Elvis Presley film, the closing scenes had both Elvis and his double turn and face the cameras; this simply clarified the absurdities that were connected with the project as a whole.

Elvis's acting in this film bordered on burlesque. He appeared to slip a notch or two down from previous form. The material with which he was working here was clearly responsible for the regression.

Overlooking any considered shortcomings, *Kissin' Cousins* was released in the US for Easter 1964, before *Viva Las Vegas*, which had been completed earlier. This occurrence did not take place in the UK, where the films were released in order.

One of the most interesting events connected with *Kissin' Cousins* was off the set and completely unknown to the public. When filming was completed, Elvis and his entourage left the location in his massive luxury mobile trailer, with Elvis himself at the wheel. Whilst driving down the Big Bear Mountain, the brakes failed on the trailer, and it simply continued to gain momentum. Without panicking and with considerable expertise, Elvis managed to get the trailer down the mountain and ran it until it stopped. His friends inside admitted that it was the most frightening experience of their lives, and had Elvis not been a superb driver, all of them would most certainly have been killed or seriously injured.

The relative cheapness of *Kissin' Cousins* was quite evident. The film was made for under $1.5 million, whereas *Blue Hawaii* had cost $4 million. Colonel Parker had won on profit, and showed complete disregard for any artistic creativity.

Roustabout

Revisiting past glories, Elvis next played a surly biker, self-assured and intensely arrogant, in the Paramount film *Roustabout*, which began filming in Thousand Oaks, California, in January 1964. There was next to no breathing space in Elvis's hectic filming schedule. He just moved from one film to another and was averaging three completed motion pictures per year.

On *Roustabout* Hal Wallis produced, and a new director for Elvis, namely John Rich, was assigned for the first of his two Presley features. Anthony Lawrence and Allan Weiss wrote the screenplay. This was the third occasion for Allan Weiss as screenwriter on an Elvis Presley–Paramount–Hal Wallis project.

Elvis had a co-star of real substance in Barbara Stanwyck, who had all but retired from the screen when she was persuaded to take this part. As Maggie, the strong-willed and determined carnival boss, she lent her distinctive style in superlative fashion. Much of the screen time between Elvis and Ms Stanwyck was spent in conflict, and their initial distrust of each other was impressively portrayed. In a film career which began in 1927, Barbara Stanwyck played in many creditworthy productions, including Billy Wilder's *Double Indemnity* (1944), and in the Hal Wallis produced *Sorry Wrong Number* (1948). For both these films, she was nominated for an Academy Award. In 1965, one year after *Roustabout*, she made her last big-screen appearance in *The Night Walker* with her ex-husband Robert Taylor. Following this she went into television work.

The redoubtable foreman of the carnival was played in typical 'heavy' style by Leif Erickson, and the love interest was provided by Joan Freeman who was surprisingly unglamorous compared to previous leading ladies. Steve Brodie appeared briefly in more or less the same role he had played in *Blue Hawaii* – that of an antagonistic know-all. All this concerted aggression led to several fight scenes, and in fact Elvis received a bad cut above his eye on the set.

Fortunately, and unlike the previous Paramount film, the use of stand-ins was minimized. For the 'wall of death' motorcycle scene, however, an experienced bike rider had to be employed. It is interesting to note that this scene formed the basis for the story of the delightful 1986 Irish film *Eat the Peach*, directed by Peter Ormrod. In that film, an unemployed man watches *Roustabout* on video tape in his local pub, and is inspired to spend his time building a 'wall of death' in his own vegetable patch.

Roustabout cast Elvis in something of a return to his pre-army characterizations. He was a moody individualist with a definite air of menace in his personality.

In the story Elvis is cast as Charlie Rogers, a wandering nightclub singer who, by accident (literally, since his motorcycle has been run off the road), meets up with some

A leather-clad biker in conflict with all around him. His adversary this time was the craggy Leif Erickson.
ROUSTABOUT

carnival people, and reluctantly agrees to work as a 'roustabout' (odd-job man), until his bike has been repaired. The carnival boss, Maggie Morgan (Barbara Stanwyck) disapproves of, but overlooks, his abrasive manner. The indomitable foreman, Joe Lean (Leif Erickson) displays total hatred for Charlie, especially when he shows interest in his (Joe's) daughter Cathy (Joan Freeman).

Charlie's enthusiasm for carnivals is non-existent and he incurs the wrath of several 'carnies' along the way. After a fight with Joe, he joins another carnival as an entertainer, receiving a substantial fee. When Maggie's carnival is about to close down due to bankruptcy, Charlie returns to swear his undying love for Cathy and to re-establish his status there in an effort to save the troubled carnival.

The plot was well enough constructed and provided some fine dramatic moments. Where it lost a great deal of credibility, however, was in the closing scenes. Elvis returns after a spell away from the carnival, and we are then to believe that the impending bankruptcy will be a thing of the past and that financial stability will reign, simply because he has been re-employed there. This can only be put down to a typical Hollywood ending of the time. Elvis Presley's films certainly did not reflect real life. 'Kitchen sink' drama, or at least its American equivalent, had not yet taken off in a big way. Escapism was still very much the working formula in Hollywood.

The soundtrack music with one or two exceptions was up to the expected standard, although in a strange move (or non-move as was the case) no single release was taken from the soundtrack album. There were several songs which could have been chosen for this, like the excellent 'Little Egypt' or 'Hard Knocks'. This was the first film since *Kid Galahad* not to have a single released from it. The album, however, received a Gold Record for sales surpassing one million dollars, so RCA would have been more than satisfied.

Some of the dialogue in the film was pretty sharp, and over all, the finished production helped to sway a certain amount of the criticism in Elvis's favour, previously at rock bottom, mostly due to mistakes like *Kissin' Cousins*. Critics, however,

104

were still regarding Elvis as someone who could no longer be taken seriously in the film business. This was an unfair charge, but it was at this time that Elvis and Colonel Parker should have been searching for another film property in the vein of *Flaming Star*. Eventually they did, but it proved to be several films too late.

Sadly, co-stars of the calibre of Barbara Stanwyck were rarely to be seen in future Elvis Presley films. Had he appeared with other leading players and acted in films with more dramatic material, then this would have allayed the criticism that he had to some extent been responsible for bringing his own way.

Roustabout was a fairly well-written story, although the improbable ending was a distinct disappointment. The soundtrack could have been shorn of several songs, thereby giving the entire production a much more dramatic flavour. Elvis's performance in the film, if not quite exemplary, was very acceptable and displayed, probably for the last time, that the non-conformist type of role was his genuine forte as a cinema actor.

From this point on, Elvis's films would show little depth, and the reasons for his admitted boredom and frustration would become obvious.

Girl Happy

Elvis returned to MGM in the summer of 1964 to film *Girl Happy*, a lively frolicsome vehicle concerning the college set. The action took place in Fort Lauderdale, Florida, a background which naturally provided much scope for numerous escapades.

Yet another directorial first assignment on an Elvis Presley film went this time to Boris Sagal. The producer was Hungarian-born Joe Pasternak, who had among his credits the classic 1939 comedy western *Destry Rides Again* with James Stewart and Marlene Dietrich and the 1945 Sinatra–Kelly musical *Anchors Aweigh*. The screenplay was written by Harvey Bullock and R.S. Allen, whilst the music was again attributed to George Stoll.

This was the first occasion since *GI Blues* in which Elvis portrayed the leader of a musical combo. He had able comic support from the other three players in the form of Gary Crosby (son of Bing), Joby Baker and Jimmy Hawkins. Hawkins would go on to play a similar role with Elvis in the 1966 film *Spinout*. The love interest was supplied by not one but two female co-stars, Shelley Fabares and Mary Ann Mobley, who would also appear in future films with Elvis. Harold J. Stone gave a good performance as Miss Fabares' tough but concerned father, and former child star Jackie Coogan made a brief appearance as a police sergeant in the film.

In the story Elvis is cast as Rusty Wells, who fronts a successful four-man combo. They move from snow-bound Chicago to the glorious sunshine of Fort Lauderdale, Florida, where they have to secretly chaperone Valerie Frank (Shelley Fabares) under threat from her aggressive father, Big Frank (Harold J. Stone), who just happens to be their present employer. Rusty meets the delectable Deena (Mary Ann Mobley) and finds himself constantly distracted from his attendant duties as a result. With her friends, Valerie gets involved in several exploits, and has to be extricated each time, unbeknownst to her, by Rusty and his friends.

Eventually Rusty is drawn to Valerie and this infuriates Deena. Rusty's attempts at reconciliation are rebuffed. Valerie again mixes with the wrong crowd and winds up in jail along with a horde of other females. Her anxious father arrives from Chicago with two purposes in mind – to find his daughter, and personally to tear Rusty and his band apart. But after an emotional explanation from Valerie, he realizes that she and Rusty have fallen in love and helps to arrange their reconciliation.

The action in the film never lets up. It is full of very engaging comedy, and Elvis again looks totally at ease with the material. Some of the frivolous exploits are hilarious, with the scene in the jail standing out. This is Elvis's only screen appearance in 'drag', complete with feminine voice, and it is very amusing.

Girl Happy was made at the time of absolute mania surrounding the Beatles; when they were at their peak as idols, and had taken the world, America especially, by storm. Perhaps it was no coincidence that suddenly Elvis was in a film which featured a four-piece band – three guitarists, bass included, and a drummer. The Beatles were considered by music pundits as a serious threat to Elvis, but at no time were there ever any real problems of competition. Such was Elvis's regard for their formidable talent that he recorded several of their songs, and also included their music in his live concert appearances.

The music for *Girl Happy* was light and enjoyable. Nothing on the soundtrack could be considered gutsy rock. One of the ballads was a beautiful song called 'Puppet on a String' written by Sid Tepper and Roy C. Bennett, two writers who had composed many songs for Elvis. The song 'Do The Clam' was released as the promotional single from the film, and reached number nine in April 1965. The 'Clam' was a strange, almost ritualistic dance and was seen performed in the film by Elvis and several other people.

The whole pace of the film was highly energetic, and this exciting atmosphere came across very well to the audience. If, in the structure of all of Elvis's light-hearted romps, this verve could have been maintained, then considerably fewer

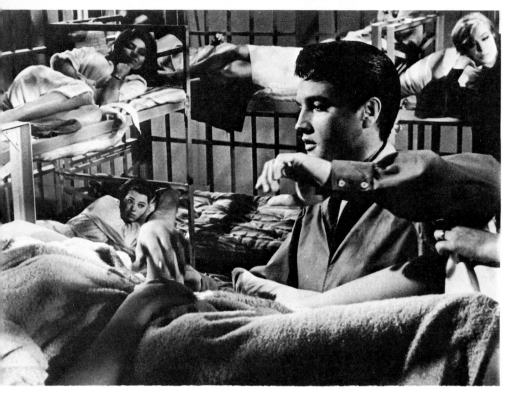

Left: An engaging and fast-paced musical comedy. This sequence led to Elvis Presley's only ever appearance in drag. *Below*: Elvis, about to be pressurized by Harold J. Stone into becoming Shelley Fabares' reluctant chaperone.
GIRL HAPPY

scathing comments would have been levelled in his direction. Unfortunately, this was not the case. Quality scripts were far from frequent in Elvis's film output.

Girl Happy presented Elvis Presley in fine physical form. He wore sleek, colourful clothes, and the 'kiss curl' styling of his hair, which had first been witnessed in *Roustabout*, was more obvious here.

Taking this as an example of musical change, the Elvis of 1964 was far removed from the raw, earthy singer who had entered the professional music world with his first Sun label record 'That's Alright Mama' in 1954. His voice had matured and developed noticeably since those early days, and the music itself had, in that first important decade, lost much of its primordial excitement.

For his mid-sixties image, *Girl Happy* was tailor-made for Elvis. He performed with his expected professional flair, and the film was yet another financial success for MGM.

Tickle Me

Moving into the arena of the modern-day western, Elvis's next film was *Tickle Me*, made in late 1964 for the financially unstable Allied Artists Picture Corporation.

Bronc-busting, women-chasing, rodeo-riding screen characters were obviously a popular attraction in the cinema, as other leading actors appeared in such roles. In 1971, James Coburn had his chance in *The Honkers*. In 1972, Cliff Robertson directed and starred in *J.W. Coop* and in the same year Steve McQueen was seen as the titular *Junior Bonner*, directed by Sam Peckinpah. These films from the early seventies were all of a reasonably serious nature, whereas *Tickle Me* was far more of a light-hearted affair.

Norman Taurog directed, and the job of producer went to Ben Schwalb. The screenplay was written by Elwood Ullman and Edward Bernds.

Elvis's leading lady was the attractive Jocelyn Lane, who provided the requisite glamour but whose acting ability left a great deal to be desired. Julie Adams, a survivor from many fifties films, played the wealthy, seductive ranch owner. The heavy of the piece was rather over-played by Edward Faulkner, a veteran of several John Wayne movies. For comic relief, the excellent and much underused Jack Mullaney played the hapless Stanley, whose heart, but unfortunately not his brain, was in the right place. He performed with a zest that served to inject the film with above-average humour.

In the story, Elvis is Lonnie Beale, a down-on-his-luck rodeo rider, who (as with many of his screen endeavours) reluctantly agrees to work on a ranch. The 'ranch' turns out to be a health farm for actresses, models and suchlike. Lonnie rooms with the zany Stanley Potter (Jack Mullaney) who attests to the good in everyone. Upon meeting the PT instructress Pam Merritt (Jocelyn Lane), Lonnie pursues her only to find that she is acutely unresponsive, resulting in his gross displeasure. The affluent owner of the ranch, Vera Radford (Julie Adams), attempts to seduce the wearisome

This sequence, with the beautiful Jocelyn Lane, did not appear in the finished film.
TICKLE ME

111

cowboy, with negative results. Lonnie has his heart set on Pam, who is indifferent to his amorous advances. Pam is attacked by an intruder and Lonnie saves her from harm. She discloses that she is the sole heir to a long-hidden treasure. Dismissing Lonnie as just another gold-digger, Pam attempts to find the gold herself in the ghost town of Silverado. Discovering that this is a most dangerous enterprise, she reluctantly enlists the assistance of Lonnie and Stanley. Challenged by several considerable foes who are all after the treasure themselves, Lonnie overcomes each hurdle as it arises. Stanley unwittingly discovers the lost gold, after which Pam sees in Lonnie more than just a wandering cowboy. They are married and leave the ranch to begin a new life together.

The plot, with its elements of farce, could hardly be considered as totally original. With a ghost town and haunted hotel in the story, it was reminiscent in essence of several Bob Hope vehicles of the 1940s.

The fact that the film was produced on a frugal budget was obvious in many ways. The outdoor background sets looked unrealistic at times and some interior shots suffered from the same fate. The many fight scenes which were included did not appear to be as skilfully choreographed as before. From any point of view, economical stringency should not have affected this particular facet of the filming.

The most notable reduction in cost outlay, which was not in any case too detrimental to the production, was in the soundtrack music used. Nine songs were performed by Elvis in the film and all of them were previous recordings. Not one new song was written or recorded for the film. Elvis did sing part of a newer version of the song 'I Feel That I've Known You Forever' which has yet to be heard on record. The choice of songs was quite impressive, ranging from the upbeat 'Night Rider' and 'Dirty Dirty Feeling' to the more mellow 'I'm Yours'. The dream sequence which featured the song 'Put the Blame on Me' was nicely done. In the same dream episode, which took us back to the Old West, a gunfight ends with Elvis shooting the villain's hand and using a band aid (a

The ghost town setting gave the film the air of a forties Bob Hope comedy.
TICKLE ME

modern contrivance in a period western sequence!) on the wound. This provided a neat parody of dramatic saloon confrontations in westerns.

A well-placed example of self-mockery is displayed when Julie Adams, questioning Elvis on how he had 'disarranged' the schedule at the ranch states: 'We're going to have to do something about your singing!' Elvis replies: 'I've been trying for years.' It is interesting and indeed admirable that he would allow himself to be sent up in this way.

The final scenes in the haunted hotel, with minor shock moments, are very amusing, and kept the audience suitably on edge. This helped to make viewers overlook the strict budget control of the production.

The success of *Tickle Me* served to steer Allied Artists away from closure for a further year. This clearly indicated the power of Elvis as a box-office crowd puller, despite the enormous criticism which came his way.

With Elvis Presley's eighteenth film in the can, Colonel Parker was well pleased.

4 Period of Stagnation (1965–67)

Hey, there were some pretty funny things in this script. I'm gonna have to read it some day.

Elvis Presley speaking to a director
after completion of one of his MGM films.

Harum Scarum (Harem Holiday)

January of 1965 saw work commence on Elvis's next project for MGM studios, *Harum Scarum* (which later, for no particular reason, became *Harem Holiday* for its UK release). This film was something of an anachronism. The progressive changes of the late-fifties film industry had all but signalled the end for swashbuckling costume pictures. For Elvis to be involved in such a venture as late as 1965 suggests that even less care was now being taken when selecting scripts for consideration.

The film was made by the same team who had already produced the inferior *Kissin' Cousins* – Gene Nelson, director; Sam Katzman, producer, and Gerald Drayson Adams, screenwriter. For Adams, this was very much a case of *déjà vu*, because *Harum Scarum* was nothing more than a Tony Curtis swashbuckler with songs. It took a mere eighteen days to shoot.

It is considered by critics and fans alike to be Elvis's worst ever film. Loyal fans told of walking out of the theatre before the end. Such reports were a heavy indication that Elvis was following a disastrous cinematic path. What was conspicuously absent from this mid-sixties period of intense film-making was the participation of film industry luminaries. Where

115

notable Academy Award-winning writers, producers, co-stars and so on were employed on previous projects, Elvis was now having to contend with people who were either fresh from television work, or who, quite simply, were lacking in talent.

Colonel Parker's motives in this respect were always patently obvious. He made no apologies for the fact that he was only interested in huge profits. What is inexcusable is the way that Elvis himself agreed to appear in such films, which he must have recognized as being potentially very harmful to his career. He later admitted to being bored stiff during the making of a number of movies, yet the fact remains that he accepted the assignments in the first place. People on the defence always state that he was signed to a contract and had little or no individual control. Perhaps this was true to a certain extent, but when he was quoted as saying to friends, regarding a script, 'What do they expect me to do with shit like this?', then surely it was time to make a personal stand, and decide on his own future.

In a June 1972 press conference in New York when asked why he was now so available as a public performer, Elvis started his answer thus: 'Just as soon as I got out of the movie contracts ...' This reply makes it seem as if he was a prisoner within a cocooned Hollywood and that he was now expressing grateful relief upon his 'release'. The sad reality is that Elvis did not, or perhaps could not, make any obvious attempt to alleviate his predicament.

In the story Elvis plays Johnny Tyronne, who (like Elvis himself) is a motion-picture and recording artist. He is kidnapped during a personal tour of the Middle East. He manages to escape from his captors, but his life is fraught with danger as he attempts to return to the Western world. He encounters the beautiful Princess Shalimar (Mary Ann Mobley) who is disguised as a slave girl, and is helped in his flight by Zacha (Jay Novello), the leader of a strange band of market-place thieves. The greedy Zacha demands payment for each and every form of assistance to Johnny. The reason for Johnny's abduction is that a group of assassins wish to employ his talents as a karate expert to kill a ruling monarch. They have been made aware of his skills at a world premiere showing of his latest film *Sands of the Desert* in which he supposedly kills a leopard with karate.

The scheming Prince Dragna (Michael Ansara) is in fact responsible for ordering the execution of his brother King Toranshah (Philip Reed), in a bid to take over the throne himself. The evil Aishah (Fran Jeffries) is also involved in this 'takeover bid'. With the aid of Zacha's many henchmen, Johnny defeats the assassins and saves the king. Shalimar and Johnny have fallen in love, and they return to the United States along with Zacha's motley crew, where they all watch Johnny perform in cabaret in Las Vegas.

One obvious plan with *Harum Scarum* was to capitalize on a sport in which Elvis was, in real life, highly proficient. The opening of the story showed the film-within-a-film sequence in which he kills the leopard. One strange point is that although numerous references were made to this 'skill with his hands' (and other euphemisms), the word 'karate' was never mentioned.

Elvis's army days had generated initial interest in karate and by 1964 he was an accomplished black belt. Karate was used in many of Elvis's films before it became a cinema genre, but Red West claimed that it was too fast for cameras to catch properly. Later martial arts films would employ much use of slow-motion techniques.

Elvis developed an all-consuming passion for karate and by 1974 had become an eighth degree ('dan' in the UK) black belt. That same year he began work on a film documentary on the subject and was to be the producer. However, it was never completed. Ed Parker, Elvis's close friend and mentor, and himself a tenth degree black belt, stated that had Elvis not been a phenomenally successful showbusiness star, he would have happily accepted the opportunity to become a full-time karate instructor. Parker added that Elvis was very adept and that he would have had no hesitation in employing him as one of his own instructors. Almost all of Elvis's stage-wear from 1969 onwards was designed from karate

The film-within-a-film opening sequence. This was considered a Valentino-type role. The anachronisms in the film were partly responsible for its being deemed Elvis Presley's worst ever. *Below*: At thirty years of age Elvis was still appearing in juvenile productions surrounded by females. It was clearly time for him to change direction in screen roles, but constant financial success delayed any risk-taking ventures. HARUM SCARUM (HAREM HOLIDAY)

suits, and on stage he often spoke of the art and in fact included entertaining demonstrations in his performance.

On a later film set Elvis explained, 'It's something I don't talk about much, because I don't want to give kids the wrong idea. It's not a sport, it's a deadly form of self-defence. I took it up in the army because I liked the idea of a mental and physical discipline.'

The music for *Harum Scarum* was recorded, incredibly, in Nashville. The musicians there must have reserved judgement for the material that they were backing. It was not quite the worst choice of songs that Elvis had ever recorded, but it came close.

There were nine songs performed in the film. One redeeming song was a powerful plaintive ballad called 'So Close Yet So Far'. Two other songs 'Animal Instinct' and 'Wisdom of the Ages' were included on the soundtrack album as bonuses (although it has been reported that prints of the film, containing these two songs, have been seen in other countries). Why they should have been excluded from US and UK versions of the film remains a mystery.

Elvis's co-stars in the film seemed less professional than previous players. Mary Ann Mobley, as the disguised princess, was ineffectual and several other supporting players appeared to be overacting. Elvis himself gave a performance from which it was difficult to tell if he was taking any of it seriously. Indeed, Elvis's comments to director Gene Nelson – 'Maybe one day we'll do one right' – seems to sum up his attitude. Considering the material, this was an understandable situation.

Physically, Elvis was in top form. He had just turned thirty years of age shortly before commencing work on the film. This was a time when he should have considered a different avenue *vis-à-vis* choice of scripts, but alas, it was not yet to be.

119

Frankie and Johnny

In spring 1965 United Artists employed Elvis for the third time for their production *Frankie and Johnny*, based on the famous folk-song of the riverboat duo. The director was Frederick de Cordova and the producer was Edward Small. The screenplay was written by Alex Gottlieb from a story by Nat Perrin.

This film was greatly enhanced by the appearance of the personable Donna Douglas (of 'Beverly Hillbillies' fame) and the excellent comic performance of Harry Morgan, as Elvis's close friend and piano player. Harry Morgan was a seasoned character actor who had performed in such classics as William Wellman's *The Ox-Bow Incident* (1943) and Fred Zinnemann's *High Noon* (1952), among others. His contribution to Elvis's latest project was a bonus. The seductive Nancy Kovack made a very glamorous Nellie Bly.

Robert Strauss, who had appeared in *Girls! Girls! Girls!*, was quite effective as a loyal but naive lackey. Anthony Eisley (of the sixties 'Hawaiian Eye' television series) featured nicely as the abrasive boss of the riverboat, with whom Elvis was frequently at odds. Sue Ane Langdon, who had earlier appeared as the wise-cracking fortune teller in *Roustabout*, was highly engaging as the love-starved Mitzi. She was involved in some splendid comic moments.

Almost all of the screen time took place on the riverboat, and it was indeed an extremely colourful atmosphere. Apart from the two westerns that Elvis had made thus far, *Frankie and Johnny* marked his first venture into a 'period' film, and the settings were impressively elaborate.

In the story Elvis is cast as Johnny, one half of a successful riverboat singing duo. He has a great love for his partner Frankie (Donna Douglas) and unfortunately also has an unquenchable propensity for gambling. All of his earnings are simply thrown away at the gaming tables. This weakness is looked upon by Frankie with evident disdain. Johnny is in debt and also in constant trouble with his boss, Clint Braden

A period musical based on the old title song. The excellent Harry Morgan made a very appealing foil as Elvis's friend.
FRANKIE AND JOHNNY

(Anthony Eisley). He is also unpopular with Braden's faithful aide Blackie (Robert Strauss). His few friends come in the form of his piano player Cully (Harry Morgan) and Cully's wife Peg (Audrey Christie). Through one misfortune after another Johnny continues gambling away his money. As the words in the song tell us, his luck changes when into his life comes a beautiful redhead called Nellie Bly, who also just happens to be a former flame of Braden's. Johnny is torn between his love for Frankie and his need for Nellie as a lucky mascot. Braden eventually senses that there is something taking place between Johnny and Nellie and for a while he consoles himself in the company of the always available Mitzi (Sue Ane Langdon). His rage over the

121

situation reaches the stage where, after a furious fist fight with Johnny, his loyal servant Blackie arranges for the singer to be shot during the production number 'Frankie and Johnny' which the duo are now performing. As a feature of their act, Frankie shoots Johnny using blank bullets – not realizing on this occasion that the obsequious and misguided Blackie has substituted live ammunition.

Johnny is saved from injury by a lucky charm that Frankie had given to him. The stark realization of all this foolishness reaches everyone and they come to their senses. Braden and Nellie are to be married, and Johnny finally realizes that the only lucky mascot he will ever really need is Frankie.

The plot was even more light-hearted than previous ventures. There was hardly one out of the film's eighty-seven minutes that could be considered as serious in any way. The jealousy which evolves out of the innocent *ménage à trois* in the story provides some sharp dialogue in the script. Harry Morgan was given most of the best lines in the film and carried them off exceptionally well.

The music, laid down in the Radio Recorders studios in Hollywood, was positively vibrant, with a distinctive jazz feel. The soundtrack even included a medley of 'Down by the Riverside' and 'When the Saints Go Marching in', both with wild hand-clapping arrangements.

The single release from the film was the title song backed with a lovely ballad from the soundtrack called 'Please Don't Stop Loving Me'. It achieved a high of number nineteen in the charts in April 1966. As a point of interest, the version of 'Frankie and Johnny' released on record was very different to the version in the film. This was nothing new, of course, and had occurred in many of Elvis's movies, including his very first, *Love Me Tender*, when an extra verse of the title song was included in the song as performed at the close of the film.

The compulsive gambler who wins and loses in love and money. Donna Douglas was a lively co-star.
FRANKIE AND JOHNNY

123

It was now well over three years since Elvis had last reached the coveted number one spot with a soundtrack single – the quality of songs was simply not good enough.

On the set of *Frankie and Johnny*, Elvis was photographed handing over a cheque for $50,000 to Frank Sinatra, who was accepting it on behalf of the Motion Picture Relief Fund – an organization that helped the many unemployed within the film industry.

Comments were made that Elvis looked noticeably over-weight for the first time on screen. This of course later proved to be an ongoing problem for him, but it was never serious in any of his films. It always looked more like puppy fat than obesity. Elvis was said to be very conscious of his weight and it no doubt bothered him that remarks about his physique were now being made.

Frankie and Johnny, for all its lightweight content, was an enjoyable musical and served well as public entertainment.

Paradise, Hawaiian Style

It was back to his beloved Hawaii for Elvis in the summer of 1965 for Paramount's *Paradise, Hawaiian Style*, his twenty-first feature film.

This was to be Elvis's penultimate film for Paramount, and his producer, as always with that studio, was Hal Wallis. Making his directorial debut was Michael Moore, who had been first assistant director on several other Elvis Presley features. The screenplay was written by Allan Weiss and Anthony Lawrence from a story by the former.

Elvis's co-stars were not particularly notable, and did little to enliven what was clearly a below-average story. From England, the attractive Suzanna Leigh was cast in the main female role. Others included Marianna Hill, who some years later appeared in a better role in Clint Eastwood's *High Plains Drifter* (1972). James Shigeta played Elvis's friend and partner in the film, and a child actress Donna Butterworth, landed a role as Shigeta's daughter and a devotee of Elvis. She sang a duet with Elvis and (albeit badly) a complete song on her own.

The promotional by-line for the film read 'Remember Blue Hawaii?', which was an all too obvious attempt to capitalize on the earlier film's huge success. But despite the breathtaking scenery, this return to the islands was a very inferior trip.

Alongside *Harum Scarum*, this film generally ranks as one of Elvis's worst. Whoever's inability to secure good scripts – Elvis's? Colonel Parker's? – was really telling by this stage. Elvis had now spent seven years, between 1956 and 1965 (two of those years were entirely devoted to the army) as a film star, completing twenty-one films in that period, an average of three motion pictures a year. As such, it was far too many, far too soon. It would be almost impossible to make twenty-one *good* films in that time for any star. Elvis Presley was no different, yet he failed to see the damage that was being done.

A conference prior to
shooting.
PARADISE, HAWAIIAN STYLE

In the story Elvis is cast as Rick Richards, a pilot who
operates a helicopter charter service with his friend Danny
Kohana (James Shigeta). For a price they will fly anyone to
anywhere, however remote, on the islands. This new
business leads them into various difficulties and they
eventually fall foul of everyone, from the Federal Aviation
authorities to the Pineapple Pickers Union. Rick's problem is
that girls will just not leave him alone no matter how diligent
he may be in his work. (If ever a time was required for new
scriptwriters, this was it.)

The partners enlist the secretarial services of Judy Hudson
(Suzanna Leigh) and in time Rick becomes attracted to her.
Danny's daughter Jan (Donna Butterworth) dotes on 'Uncle
Rick' and spends considerable time with him. With the help
of several island acquaintances (all female) Rick secures a
fair amount of clients. The helpful girls all request the
pleasure of his company in return, and Rick finds great
difficulty in trying to make himself available. He is grounded

following an incident involving some out-of-control dogs, but when he later rescues the stricken Danny from a helicopter accident, he is granted permission to resume flying. The native girls, becoming aware of each others' interest in Rick, resolve not to mix business with pleasure. He now candidly expresses his feelings for Judy.

The music, again recorded in Hollywood, where Elvis and the production team would be doing interiors for the film, was pleasant and produced one or two surprises. It was, however, vastly inferior to the *Blue Hawaii* soundtrack. Where this first album had been released with fourteen songs, the stingy RCA executives gave record buyers a mere ten track album. One of these ten tracks 'Sand Castles', was recorded for the film but, suffering the same fate as others before, was cut from the final print. The inexplicable part of this decision is that it was a far superior song than many of those left intact. Another song, 'Now is the Hour', was said to have been recorded for the film, although no trace of this can be found among Elvis's listed discography.

On the set of the film in Honolulu, Elvis met with the then popular Herman's Hermits, a teen-oriented group from England. An awkward-sounding interview was recorded between Elvis and lead singer Peter Noone, arranged by one Tom Moffett, and was subsequently available on record. The strange part of this conversation is that Elvis appears to understand everything Peter Noone is saying, whereas Noone keeps asking Elvis to repeat himself, apologizing meanwhile for not being able to understand his accent.

The questions are hardly intriguing, and consist mostly of the stock questions Elvis was being asked throughout the 1960s (on the rare occasions when he granted interviews). 'When are you coming to Britain?' was, even by that time, more of a cliché than it was a true question. Elvis, as ever, deftly answered that by saying that really the decision is up to Colonel Parker, thereby dismissing the issue as one of his own responsibilities.

Whilst in Hawaii, Elvis revisited the site of the monument to the USS *Arizona*, for whose fund he had performed a concert in 1961. Elvis had a definite affinity with the people

127

Over the years, Elvis developed an affinity with the Hawaiian people, who warmly welcomed him back for a satellite concert in 1973.
PARADISE, HAWAIIAN STYLE

of Hawaii, and although he did not return there to make any further feature films, he did visit fairly frequently.

What the studios undoubtedly hoped for – a blockbuster equal to *Blue Hawaii* – was of course never realized, but *Paradise, Hawaiian Style* was still a comfortable financial success. In a 1966 interview Colonel Parker said: 'People say Elvis's pictures aren't doing so good. I tell you we've made twenty-two pictures and nineteen have been big box-office successes; two haven't yet completed their runs, and one hasn't yet been released. If his pictures aren't so successful, how come all the people who made 'em want him for more? *Paradise, Hawaiian Style* hasn't finished forty per cent of its run yet, but Hal Wallis called me this morning to say how happy he was with receipts and to discuss the next one.'

Who indeed could argue with this logic?

However, even if sufficient crowds were still attending showings of Elvis Presley films, there was still a diminishing trend, quite apart from the question of quality, reflected in the fact that he had not bettered, nor indeed maintained, the level of financial success attributed to the likes of *Blue Hawaii*. And, the intransigence of studio executives was creating increasingly damaging effects.

Perhaps it did not seem futile to have Elvis return to Hawaii. After all, it was a splendrous location, filled with obvious beauty, and a wealth of situations could be concocted there.

What emerged was an example of below-average cinema fare, with a lukewarm performance from a probably bored Elvis. There was again the annoying over-use of stand-ins. Maybe, Elvis was so disillusioned that he simply refused to do certain scenes – hence the stand-in. Perhaps not. Whichever way, one gets the distinct feeling that Elvis was pleased to see this film behind him.

Spinout (California Holiday)

Following the trip to Hawaii, Elvis had a brief hiatus from his furious film-making, and for the remainder of 1965 he stayed away from the studios.

In February 1966 he was back at MGM studios to begin work on *Spinout*, his second and last involvement with producer Joe Pasternak. Norman Taurog directed, and the screenplay was written by Theodore J. Flicker and George Kirgo.

The story was originally conceived as a vehicle for Sonny and Cher, but this project was dropped. In altering the structure of the plot, the writers included a racing-car theme, and so for the second time Elvis found himself in the role of racing driver. In this story he also just happened to be the leader of a combo constantly harassed by women. Throughout the film, he frequently makes claims about his desire to remain single, but three different females have other plans for his status.

Shelley Fabares, in her second Presley film, played the spoiled daughter of a wealthy businessman, who is in turn a rival to Elvis on the track. Carl Betz took the role of Elvis's automotive opponent. Diane McBain was cast as a writer in the Jackie Collins mould – a successful author of several controversial and *risqué* novels.

Deborah Walley played the third opportunistic woman, as well as the tomboyish drummer in the band. Jimmy Hawkins from *Girl Happy* again played a band member, as did Jack Mullaney from *Tickle Me*. Mullaney was less effective here, though, than he had been in the earlier film. Will Hutchins from the television series 'Tenderfoot' played a policeman. A good comic performance was elicited from Warren Berlinger as an excitable hypochondriac in the employ of Carl Betz.

The affluent elderly couple who befriend Elvis in the film were delightfully played by Una Merkel and Cecil Kellaway. Una Merkel had a long film career and in 1961 was nominated for an Oscar for her role in Hal Wallis's production of *Summer and Smoke*, from the Tennessee Williams play. South African-born Cecil Kellaway also had a long and distinguished film career, receiving two Academy Award nominations for best supporting actor. The first occasion was in *The Luck of the Irish* in 1947, which was written by Philip Dunne, the man who would later direct Elvis in *Wild in the Country*. Kellaway's second nomination came towards the close of his career in Stanley Kramer's *Guess Who's Coming to Dinner* (1967).

Having performers of this calibre in the cast certainly improved the acting standards in *Spinout*, although the plot was rather foolish and detracted from the high-quality contribution.

In the story Elvis is Mike McCoy, a free-wheeling singer with his own combo which travels up and down the country. Mike is also a successful racing driver and divides his time between both pursuits. In Santa Barbara, California, the band meet tycoon Howard Foxhugh (Carl Betz) and his outrageously pampered daughter Cynthia (Shelley Fabares). Mike and his friends are moving on to their next booking when the influential Foxhugh arranges to cancel their tour, forcing them to return to his home town to sing just one song for his daughter's birthday. The disgusted and enraged band reluctantly go through with the changed booking. Onto the scene comes authoress Diana St Clair (Diane McBain), who is completing her latest book *The Perfect American Male*. She decides that Mike fits the bill and that therefore they should both be married. Cynthia, meanwhile, feels the same towards Mike and sets out to capture him for herself.

Les (Deborah Walley), the drummer in the band, also has designs on Mike, who fails to notice. In an effort to hit back at the powerful Foxhughs, Mike charms the elderly Ranleys (Una Merkel and Cecil Kellaway) into letting him and his friends reside in their home – right next door to the Foxhughs.

Race time, meanwhile, is drawing near, and Mike refuses to drive Foxhugh's new 'Fox 5' super racing-car, preferring to attempt the race in a vehicle of his own choice. Foxhugh's aide, Philip Short (Warren Berlinger), a loyal but easily

Above: Intent on success in his second racing film.
Right: The portrayal of winners was very much the
Hollywood maxim during this period.

SPINOUT (CALIFORNIA HOLIDAY)

excitable man, detests Mike and moreover has a personal longing for Cynthia. But she fails to reciprocate his feelings having eyes only for Mike. Officer Tracy Richards (Will Hutchins) becomes attracted to Les via the passion they both share for gourmet food.

Mike narrowly wins the race and then announces that he is going to marry all three girls. This he does – but each one to a different partner – while he stays the way he wants to be: single and free.

Before its UK release at the close of 1966, the film was retitled *California Holiday*. That now made two Elvis Presley films with 'Holiday' in the title (for the UK market, that is), and in fact a working title for an earlier Paramount film was 'Holiday in Acapulco'. Fortunately it was changed. It is clear why Elvis's films were once described as travelogues.

The music was similar in style and tempo to that heard in MGM's earlier *Girl Happy* – a mixture of ballads and light rock songs. A single was issued from the soundtrack album consisting of the soft 'All that I am' and the heavier 'Spinout' songs. In October 1966 this record only reached a peak of number twenty-two. Early in the film there is a nicely-worked homage to Elvis's famous 'Hound Dog' song.

Unlike his previous films Elvis did not end up happily paired off with any of his female co-stars, which was a welcome change in the general trend. Another girl, Dodie Marshall, played a brief role in the film, and later that year would appear with Elvis in another film as a fully-fledged co-star.

Spinout was a lively, harmless, even likeable musical, better than some, worse than others. Elvis was by now deeply entrenched in a 'formula' rut and it seemed with no-one to guide him, he would continue along this path. Cinema audiences would soon indicate to him that a radical change was necessary.

Double Trouble

June of 1966 saw Elvis return to MGM studios to make *Double Trouble*. When this project was first announced, it led one to hope that Elvis was at last making a more dramatic film. The completed film unfortunately tells a different story.

Norman Taurog again directed. The screenplay was written by Jo Heims, from a story by Marc Brandel, and the producers were Judd Bernard and Irwin Winkler. Winkler formed a later partnership with Robert Chartoff and included among their successes are the enormously popular *Rocky* films with Sylvester Stallone.

The fact that the setting of the story was in Europe had people looking forward to a possible visit from Elvis to British shores. This promising thought was short-lived, however. When filming began, it was evident that Elvis was not going to set one foot out of Hollywood. As with *Fun in Acapulco*, all the settings were staged in the studio. The story opened in London, and some location filming had taken place there by a second unit crew but without the main star, of course. London and Belgium as seen in the film were simply studio-set creations.

The co-stars at least *were* European. John Williams, Yvonne Romain, Monty Landis and Norman Rossington all added a typical British flavour to the production. Norman Rossington must be the only actor to have the (dubious?) distinction of appearing in both an Elvis Presley Hollywood musical and a British-made Beatles film (*A Hard Day's Night*, 1964). Australian actor Chips Rafferty was cast as Rossington's inept partner in crime.

The main female lead was a young English girl named Annette Day who was plucked from obscurity, working in the market area of London's Portobello Road. Against all the odds, she was selected to go to Hollywood and play a major role, with no previous acting experience whatsoever. When the film was completed, she returned to that same obscurity and never acted again.

I met and spoke with Annette Day at length in April 1987, almost twenty-one years after her sole Hollywood experience. In retrospect, she said, the entire affair seemed like a far-off dream, but she remembered that Elvis had been most kind and courteous to her, almost paternal. She stated that, away from the set, she did not really see him. Her only contact was during the actual filming, but he personally arranged for her to be extremely comfortable during her stay and he gifted her with a brand new car. She remembered being completely overwhelmed by this gesture. I found it encouraging to hear her express such glowing comments about Elvis Presley. Ms Day openly reiterated her feelings regarding his charm and great generosity.

The Weire Brothers, a stage act with vaudeville origins, appeared in the film as three bungling detectives in a clear plagiarism of Peter Sellers' famous Inspector Clouseau character. Rather than adding any great comic touches to the film, they were quite superfluous.

Cast in the role of a smooth-talking hit-man was Michael Murphy, who later went on to leading roles in films like Paul Mazursky's *An Unmarried Woman* (1977), Oliver Stone's *Salvador* (1986) and several with Woody Allen. There is an extremely well-choreographed karate fight between Presley and Murphy in the film, which resulted in the latter character's death.

In the story Elvis plays Guy Lambert, a carefree singer who is currently on a tour of Europe. In London he becomes romantically involved with Jill Conway (Annette Day) whom he later discovers to be only seventeen years old and set to gain a substantial inheritance on her imminent eighteenth birthday. After a confrontation with Jill's protective uncle, Gerald Waverly (John Williams), Guy leaves on a night boat to Belgium, where he is scheduled to perform. He discovers that Jill is also on the boat, and as they prepare to disembark, Guy thwarts an attempt to kill her. Sophisticated socialite Claire Dunham (Yvonne Romain) shows interest in Guy, but with the wayward teenager's constant interference, he finds little time to become more acquainted with her.

They encounter two clumsy jewel thieves, Babcock and Brown (Norman Rossington and Chips Rafferty), who switch suitcases with the unsuspecting couple. Also conveniently on hand is Morley (Michael Murphy), a seemingly pleasant young man whom Jill innocently confides in. Further unsuccessful attempts on Jill's life are made, resulting in the appearance of three awkward detectives (The Weire Brothers) who seek to solve the mystery.

A defensive stance. This scene followed a professionally orchestrated and lengthy karate sequence involving Elvis and actor Michael Murphy.
DOUBLE TROUBLE

Morley, it transpires, is actually a contract killer, and during yet another bid to dispose of Jill, he engages in a violent contest with Guy in which he is killed.

The evil-doers who wish to get rich on Jill's inheritance turn out to be none other than her greedy uncle Gerald, who, along with Claire, was on course for a financially comfortable future. They are both promptly arrested.

Following Jill's eighteenth birthday, she and Guy are married.

Adding elements of mystery and mayhem was at least a change of pace for an Elvis Presley vehicle, but it could have been dealt with more seriously. Of his own performance in the film Elvis commented: 'I wasn't exactly a James Bond in that movie, but then no one ever asked Sean Connery to sing while dodging bullets.' Caustic words indeed.

The music in the film could only be described as, at best, average. There were no songs to enthuse over, although a very listenable ballad called 'Could I Fall in Love?' was included. 'City by Night', a jazz/blues-influenced track also had its attractions. The single release from the soundtrack album was the extremely brief 'Long-Legged Girl (with the Short Dress on)', clearly written with a view to highlighting current fashion trends. This song hit a 'high' of number forty-nine in September 1967.

By far the worst song on the soundtrack, and an embarrassing scene in the film, was 'Old Macdonald'. Could this really be Elvis Presley, the legendary rock singer, warbling about chickens, pigs and other farmyard animals? Elvis was hitting an all-time low using such material and must have felt positively ill in the recording studios. The argument still remained – why did he agree to record such feeble material? Amazingly, worse was still to come on future soundtracks. The following year, Elvis would record several film songs so stupefyingly infantile that they almost defy description.

Double Trouble had a promising start and several worthwhile moments, but ultimately proved to be a disappointment after what had been expected.

Easy Come, Easy Go

Easy Come, Easy Go, which began shooting in September 1966, was to be Elvis's final film for the Paramount – Hal Wallis production stable. The director was John Rich (from *Roustabout*) and the screenplay was written by Allan Weiss and Anthony Lawrence.

The female lead was played by Dodie Marshall, who provided a very amateur performance. Pat Harrington was cast as Elvis's musician friend, and veteran character actor Frank McHugh had a role as an eccentric captain. The almost obligatory famous name from the past who graced this particular production was Elsa Lanchester, cast as an outlandish yoga instructress (yoga was another fad very much in vogue at the time). Actor Skip Ward played Elvis's scheming adversary, and naturally they had a rousing fist fight.

In the story Elvis is Ted Jackson, a naval frogman whose job it is to deactivate old war mines. On an assignment he discovers a sunken ship which he later learns was carrying treasure. Upon his return to civilian life he pursues the idea of bringing the booty to the surface. Ted persuades his friend Judd Whitman (Pat Harrington), a musician who owns a local nightclub, to put up finance equal to his own discharge pay in an attempt to salvage the ship's riches.

The hopeful pair enlist the services of the eccentric Captain Jack (Frank McHugh), who specializes in deep-sea diving and salvage equipment. He refers them to Jo Symington (Dodie Marshall), a descendant of the sunken ship's captain. When she learns of their quest for financial gain, she is at first furious, but reluctantly offers her assistance.

Attempting to thwart their plans is the attractive Dina Bishop (Pat Priest), who, aided by her henchman Gil Corey (Skip Ward), makes her own bid to recover the treasure.

Ted and his friends finally achieve their goal, only to discover that the 'treasure' is in fact a hoard of copper coins

Above: The last film to feature Elvis dressed in military uniform. He was cast as a naval underwater expert de-activating old mines. This was also his last association with producer Hal Wallis and Paramount pictures. *Right*: The archetypal Presley pose. The soundtrack music fell well below previous standards.

EASY COME, EASY GO

which are virtually worthless. With the meagre sum of money obtained from them and the remainder of Ted's pay, they plan to put a down payment on the art centre that Jo has always dreamed of having. At Judd's nightclub a benefit event will be staged to obtain further funds. Despite the previous disappointments, Ted and Jo are now an extremely happy couple.

This was not the most original story line, and the comic content was minimal. The attempted allusions to the then prominent hippy lore were trite and contrived. It was the kind of script that dates very quickly. 'Peace and love, man' and other such banalities could not be served up as entertainment.

Had Paramount studios deigned that Allan Weiss was the only choice of screenwriter for Elvis Presley films? There must have been other worthy writers who could have constructed a different style of motion picture for him.

Elvis and his director John Rich did not see eye to eye, and in his book Sonny West related an incident where Rich screamed at the star and several others in Elvis's group of friends to leave the set because of their juvenile antics. Elvis responded to the director's outburst with a vitriolic rebuke of his own and, as a result, his friends remained on the set. This incident was in fact used in the John Carpenter bio-pic, *Elvis – The Movie*.

As was now becoming the norm, Elvis waltzed through *Easy Come, Easy Go* ostensibly unaware of the absurdities surrounding him. The only real depth in the story was that which was seen under the ocean.

The music recorded for the film was conspicuous by nothing more than its mediocrity. Six songs were featured in the film, two of which were released as a single, the remaining four making up an EP. In several other countries outside the UK the six songs were released together. The single release was the song 'The Love Machine' backed with 'You Gotta Stop'. This record was unlikely to set the charts on fire and only reached number thirty-eight by July 1967.

Another song recorded for the film was 'She's a Machine', which was cut and only later turned up on a 1969 budget album. Two other songs mentioned as having been recorded for the soundtrack were 'Leave My Woman Alone' and 'Wheel of Fortune'. To date, nothing has been heard of these tracks on record.

An odd fact surrounding the film's UK release was that it was rushed out before *Double Trouble*, which had been completed earlier. This topsy-turvy scheduling had of course taken place in 1964 with *Kissin' Cousins* and *Viva Las Vegas* in the United States.

Elvis had now completed his last Paramount contract; he had made nine films in as many years for the studio. The parting was amicable, even though Elvis would not appear in any more films for them. Of the selection of films made there, all were financially successful, some were particularly memorable and others were easily forgettable.

One man who had great cause to be satisfied over Elvis's association with Paramount was producer Hal B. Wallis. He had been an independent producer for some years and in the process of shrewdly moulding Elvis Presley into a film star had become enormously wealthy. Perhaps he deserved it for his diligence if nothing else. Reservedly one could say, however, that Hal Wallis was probably partly responsible, along with Colonel Parker, for denying Elvis Presley any challenging opportunities. Elvis himself had a deep respect for Wallis and felt that, with so many years spent in the profession, his decisions would almost certainly be the right ones. How sad, looking back, to see that this simply was not the case.

With *Easy Come, Easy Go* an era had ended for Elvis. It was unfortunate that it did not finish on a higher note, with a film of the calibre of, say, *King Creole*.

Clambake

Elvis surprised the world on 1 May 1967 when it was announced that he had married Priscilla Beaulieu in a private ceremony in Las Vegas. The newsreels of the event showed an Elvis who looked beside himself with happiness. Just weeks before the marriage, however, Elvis had begun work on his twenty-fifth feature film *Clambake*, for United Artists, and in the completed film, looked anything but content.

The director was Arthur Nadel, the producers were Jules Levy, Arthur Gardner and Arnold Laven, and the screenplay was written by Arthur Browne jun.

The younger members of the supporting cast were Shelley Fabares (in her third Presley film), Will Hutchins (in his second) and Bill Bixby. The older generation was represented by James Gregory, playing Elvis's oil-tycoon father and Gary Merrill as the owner of the boat company. Gary Merrill had some notable films to his credit including Darryl F. Zanuck's powerful 1950 classic *All About Eve* which earned a glut of Oscar nominations and Awards. Why he should have involved himself in a project like this is a mystery.

Jack Good the British impresario responsible for the 1950s 'Oh Boy' television show and instrumental in establishing Cliff Richard's career had a part in the film as the hotel manager. Just four years after making the film he described it as 'one of the really, really, awful ones', and indeed this simply had to be Elvis's worst film ever, for several reasons including, and especially the music.

In the story Elvis is cast as Scott Heyward, the son of Texas oil millionaire Duster Heyward (James Gregory). The independent Scott sets out to prove that he can survive on his own. In attempting to establish that point, he exchanges places with a water-ski instructor called Tom Wilson (Will Hutchins), assuming his routine identity as the happy-go-lucky beach boy – whilst the ecstatic instructor adopts the high life of a spoiled millionaire's son. They travel to the

144

same hotel – one residing as a pampered guest, the other merely as an employee.

Scott meets Dianne Carter (Shelley Fabares) and soon falls foul of the wealthy playboy James Jamison III (Bill Bixby) who is there to participate in the annual speedboat race, the Orange Bowl Regatta. Scott has aspirations to win this prestigious race himself and works tirelessly to perfect a substance called 'goop' that will prevent damage to a fast-moving boat. Scott achieves this, as is his intention, without any form of financial assistance from his affluent father. He has been taken under the wing of boat builder Sam Burton (Gary Merrill) who has kindly given him scope to work in his laboratory.

Race day arrives and Scott triumphs over the furious Jamison. Afterwards he makes amends with his father and reveals his true identity to a stunned Dianne, who has by this time fallen in love with him.

This was Elvis's fourth and last motion picture for United Artists. Perhaps both he and the studio parted company gladly after this cinema débâcle. Where could Elvis go from here? He seemed positively bored throughout the entire film. How else could he look in such an insipid, unimaginative vehicle?

The fun and excitement connected with this production was all entirely off-camera. Elvis's various friends have documented the outrageous antics in which they all participated on the set. Red West and some others climbed on to rafters from the old *Phantom of the Opera* set and rained down water balloons on those below, then pies filled with shaving cream. Red West once covered himself in blood to give Elvis a fright; dressing-room doors would suddenly fly open; cherry bombs would explode; and the cast would throw whole buckets of water over each other.

Unlike that of Elvis's previous film, *Clambake*'s director Arthur Nadel was himself not averse to occasional humorous diversion. An obvious indication of his good humour over such incidents was the fact that on one occasion he appeared on the set wearing a rain hat, coat and rubber boots! Indeed, following completion of the film, at the closing party, he was

145

A song-and-dance sequence with co-star Will Hutchins and several girls. Overall, the film was a backward step in Elvis's career. CLAMBAKE

involved in as much frolicsome activity as the actors. But it is regretful that this atmosphere of bonhomie was not readily apparent where it mattered most – in the finished film.

Although United Artists made this movie, the filming was done on the studio lot of Universal pictures – a kind of 'on loan' arrangement. Elvis would return to Universal two years later for his final film as an actor.

The music for the film was totally uninspired. There was a commendable ballad entitled 'The Girl I Never Loved' and the excellent 'You Don't Know Me' (co-written by country singer Eddy Arnold, and a previous hit for Ray Charles), but the soundtrack also contained two songs that should never have been written, much less recorded. One was the awful 'Confidence' sung to and with a group of children, and the other, 'Who Needs Money?' must rank as the most embarrassingly dreadful song that Elvis ever put on record. Will Hutchins joined Elvis on a motorbike for a duet, and the song, as seen performed in the film, is treated as a caricature. This was soundtrack music at its absolutely lowest level.

The remainder of the songs in the film were mostly forgettable. One called 'How Can You Lose What You Never Had?' was cut from the film, but included on the soundtrack album. No matter, it merely equalled the others in terms of musical inanity.

The best thing that can be said about *Clambake* was that from here on, Elvis could only climb back up the scale. Unfortunately, there was to be one more below-par film before his change of direction began.

Speedway

In June 1967, Elvis began filming *Speedway* for MGM. It was at least a marginal improvement on *Clambake*.

Norman Taurog directed what was to be his penultimate assignment with Elvis. The producer was Douglas Laurence and the screenplay was written by Phillip Shuken.

There were no earth-shattering co-stars on this occasion. Bill Bixby, from Elvis's previous film played his manager-friend, and the female lead was given to Nancy Sinatra, who was inexperienced in film work. This was not her first acting role but, despite the fact that she claimed Elvis and she had a wonderful chemistry working together, she looked relatively uncomfortable for most of the film. Nancy Sinatra had been a friend since Elvis's initial post-army days, and they complemented each other quite well on screen; but this was no *Viva Las Vegas* and Ms Sinatra did not possess the radiant dynamics of Ann-Margret.

Displaying absolute lack of invention regarding story lines, the producers cast Elvis as a racing driver for the third time. In comparison to *Viva Las Vegas*, *Speedway* was an abysmal tale.

In its favour, the race scenes were exciting, though perhaps too frequent. Many legitimate race-car drivers were listed in the credits including champion drivers like Tiny Lund and Cale Yarborough. The latter was still involved in film work as late as 1983 in the Burt Reynolds–Hal Needham film *Stroker Ace*.

In the story, Elvis plays Steve Grayson, a successful racing driver with extravagant tastes. He is also a great benefactor to everyone around him. If someone needs a certain something, Steve willingly foots the bill. Noble though this may be, Steve soon finds himself and his manager Kenny Donford (Bill Bixby) in deep financial trouble with the Internal Revenue Service (IRS). The gross inefficiency of his manager is the sole cause of his plight: Kenny has an uncontrollable propensity towards gambling and his luck in this endeavour fails to match his enthusiasm.

Left: Performing 'Let Yourself Go' – a well-chosen song that Elvis would use again the following year in his much-acclaimed NBC TV Special. *Below:* Looking elegant, if somewhat belligerent, at a wedding scene with co-stars Nancy Sinatra and Bill Bixby. SPEEDWAY

Susan Jacks (Nancy Sinatra) is assigned by the IRS to monitor and, if needs be, budget the earnings of the two spendthrifts. Angered by the two men's refusal to accept the seriousness of the problem, she pursues her task zealously and follows their every move.

Steve's conciliatory behaviour is initially rebuffed, but gradually the personal barriers are broken down, and a mutual attraction flourishes. Almost all of Steve's personal belongings are repossessed with the exception of his race car. In his final race, he finishes second, and that takes care of at least some of the money he owes. With the advice of Susan, his financial problems, if not solved, are now under control, and the one-time enemies are now very much in love.

The film, as much a stereotype as any other, had the usual ingredients: an assiduous adversary, a fist fight, engaging children and, of course, a climactic conclusion. If this demonstration of expected histrionics was used once, it was used a dozen times.

Elvis, at thirty-two years of age, was going nowhere fast. Singing to children and bored adults was no longer beguiling, and the material was distinctly unworthy of him. In fact, upon its release in the UK, *Speedway* shared equal billing with the final *Man From UNCLE* feature film, a fate which had not befallen any previous Elvis Presley film. In some programmes, it was in fact billed as the second feature.

The music, once again, was only slightly better than that featured in *Clambake*. There were seven songs, one of which Nancy Sinatra got to sing by herself. Two other songs, 'Five Sleepy Heads' and 'Suppose' were recorded for the film but cut from the final print. They were both included as bonus songs on the soundtrack album. The single release from the film was the catchy 'Your Time Hasn't Come Yet Baby' backed with 'Let Yourself Go'. The latter was a good production number which Elvis would re-use a year later during the taping of his legendary NBC television special. The single reached a high of number twenty-two in the charts of August 1968.

It was while filming *Speedway* that Elvis learned of Priscilla's pregnancy. He was reportedly ecstatic over this news. Nancy Sinatra, in an interview in the *New Musical Express*, stated that it was a wonderfully happy occasion for everyone making the film. In the completed film, Elvis appeared to be in great spirits, but his performance was less than enthralling. In some scenes he acted with just a hint of amateur theatrics, which made it difficult to compare this role with, say, his compelling characterization in *Flaming Star* seven years earlier.

Clambake was the first of two films made in 1967 which can only be considered as among his least satisfactory from the viewpoint of entertainment. It was also the year in which he starred in a motion picture that was for him, unintentionally or otherwise, a distinct change of image. Time would now tell if this iconoclastic exercise was merely fortuitous, or if it was a planned form of redemption.

5 *The Changing Image (1968–69)*

I realise I've come to an important cross-road in my career. I can't go on playing teenagers for ever. After all, I am 32. As for the criticism of my films – I didn't make them for the critics in the first place.

Elvis Presley on film

Stay Away, Joe

In October 1967 Elvis began work on MGM's *Stay Away, Joe* on location in Sedona, Arizona. This was the setting of many a western film, and the scenery was breathtaking. The movie was Elvis's second contemporary western and he excelled in his role as the licentious Joe Lightcloud. Whilst it may not be considered to be Elvis Presley's cinematic renaissance, it came very close to that description. The Elvis Presley of *Speedway*, just months before, seemed like another person. In this, his second portrayal of a half-breed Indian, Elvis looked bronzed and radiant. Whereas *Flaming Star* was a heavy, dramatic piece, *Stay Away, Joe* was a knockabout screwball comedy.

The director was Peter Tewksbury and the producer was Douglas Laurence (from *Speedway*). The screenplay was written by Michael A. Hoey from Dan Cushman's 1953 novel. Cushman was the author of numerous western novels, including *Four For Texas*, another serio-comic tale, which had been filmed by director Robert Aldrich in 1963 with Frank Sinatra and Dean Martin starring. Uncredited as co-writer of *Stay Away, Joe* was Burt Kennedy, talented director of successful comedy westerns such as *Support Your*

153

Local Sheriff (1968), *Dirty Dingus Magee* (1970) and *Support Your Local Gunfighter* (1971). Kennedy requested that his name be removed from the credits because of his dissatisfaction with the final script.

Elvis's co-stars were from exemplary stock. Playing his beleaguered father was seasoned character actor Burgess Meredith. Making his film debut in 1936, he had worked long and hard establishing himself as a dependable screen actor. In later years he was best known for his role as Sylvester Stallone's trainer–manager in the *Rocky* series of films.

Katy Jurado played Elvis's long-suffering, temperamental stepmother, who had no time for his largely irresponsible behaviour. She had appeared in several noteworthy films and they were mostly westerns. She was given a good role in Fred Zinnemann's *High Noon* (1952) and had gained an Academy Award nomination for her performance in Edward Dmytryk's *Broken Lance* (1954), in which she worked alongside actors like Spencer Tracy and Richard Widmark. Remaining actively in the genre, she had roles in Marlon Brando's *One-Eyed Jacks* (1961) and in Sam Peckinpah's elegiac *Pat Garrett and Billy the Kid* (1973).

On the set of *Stay Away, Joe* it was reported that she and Elvis had a great rapport and that she was knitting clothes for his soon-to-be-born child. Elvis addressed her with a very neat corruption of her own name – 'Karate Judo'.

Giving a lovely performance was veteran actor Thomas Gomez as Elvis's anachronistic grandfather. He still had notions of scalping white men and considered modern-day inventions like motor cars to be distinctly evil.

Joan Blondell, the former *Ziegfeld Follies* Girl-turned-actress, was cast as Glenda, the sharp-tongued proprietress of the local bar, with whom Joe has clearly had a past affair. Joan Blondell began her film career in 1930 and went on to receive an Academy Award nomination for her role in *The Blue Veil* (1951). Her frosty performance in *Stay Away, Joe* added much to the film's atmosphere.

Elvis's close friend in the story, Bronc, was played by L.Q. Jones, here cast in his third and final Elvis Presley film.

'A wheeler-dealer, part Hud, part Alfie' was Elvis's own description of Joe Lightcloud, the irrepressible hero of the piece.
STAY AWAY, JOE

Jones lent support in various creditable films such as Ted Post's *Hang 'em High* (1968) with Clint Eastwood and a trio of acclaimed Sam Peckinpah westerns, namely *The Wild Bunch* (1969), *The Ballad of Cable Hogue* (1970) and *Pat Garrett and Billy the Kid* (1973). Later on, he formed his own production company called LQJAF, which stood for 'L.Q. Jones and Friends', and moved into producing and directing small-budget feature films.

Elvis's friend Sonny West, normally an extra in the background, had a credited part in the film.

155

The structure of the story is a satire on the relationship and dealings between the US government and the American Indian. In the novel Joe is a Marine Corps veteran of the Korean War, with a Purple Heart and some toes missing (an injury of which he makes a great deal). He is also a champion rodeo rider, winning trophies at Madison Square Garden and other venues. The latter pursuit is the one highlighted in the film version. There is no mention of any war, medals or injuries. A song called 'Too Much Monkey Business' had been planned for the film, but was cut out. Included in that song was the line 'Been to Vietnam, been fighting in the war ...'. Perhaps the intention was to update the war theme, but possibly a decision was made to cut the theme entirely. The location was changed from Montana in the book to Arizona in the film, and the character is often referred to as 'Big Joe', since he is meant to stand about six feet 3 inches. Elvis at six foot was by no means diminutive, but not quite warranting the 'Big' prefix. Joe's surname is changed from Champlain to Lightcloud.

Despite these obvious differences, the film follows its forebear quite accurately, and is in fact less racy than the novel, both in language and sexual encounters. Some characters are missing who feature prominently in the book and Elvis's Joe is less of a con-man on screen than in the written version.

On the set Elvis had this to say in an interview, which was later published in *Reveille* in May 1969:

It's great to have money and recognition, but it really isn't enough. I guess I'd like to prove myself as an actor and, to do that, I'll have to take more chances. You can learn an awful lot just by hanging out with real good professionals, and there isn't a day that goes by that I don't pick up on something from the other actors.

Right now, I'm still taking little steps because I'm not all that sure of my ability. There's a lot more I want to do before I call myself an actor.

I look at my old movies and I can pick up on my mistakes. There's a lot I'd like to change. I want to grow up on screen. When I see my old movies, something is always happening to me, someone's always telling me what to do. Girls are chasing me. Bad guys are after me. Now I'm getting away from that.

In *Stay Away, Joe* I'm a wheeler-dealer who's always promoting something. It's a more grown-up character – part Hud, part Alfie.

He's a man, not a boy, and he's out looking for women, not just waiting for them to stumble over him. In most of my pictures, I'm singing in every other scene, but in this one I do only three songs and I get to do a lot more acting. There isn't a guitar in the whole picture.

Of his stunts and fight scenes in the film he said: 'This ain't a picture, it's a fight for survival.' This referred to the many action scenes in which he was involved.

In a 1968 article, from a now-defunct movie magazine, entitled 'Can Presley K.O. his Critics?' the director of *Stay Away, Joe*, Peter Tewksbury, had this to say: 'There is far more drama in this picture. Elvis responded marvellously to direction. He may not be thought of as a serious actor, but he could teach one or two so-called serious actors a thing or two.'

Not everyone concurred, however. One book reviewer had this to say: 'Elvis films on and on; incredibly some of his pictures are based on novels. I could visualize a good production coming from Dan Cushman's *Stay Away, Joe*; a fun story of a mod Indian with a great thirst for flash cars and women. He rushes about like the last of the free men. Now, alas, he's going to have to sing like one, too.'

Film reviewer Leslie Halliwell, in typically belittling fashion, could only comment: 'Thin if surprising vehicle for a singing star; all rather tedious.'

The music consisting of only a few songs, was incidental. There was no single release from the film. A very good song, entitled 'Going Home' was recorded for the film, but cut out. It appeared as a bonus song on the *Speedway* soundtrack album. The bluesy 'All I Needed was the Rain' was a welcome inclusion in the film. 'Dominic', a strange song about a bull, was more of a novelty.

The film version of the story has Joe returning from the rodeo circuit to his family home. He has arranged, through an aspiring congressman (Douglas Henderson), for his father

One step ahead of irate boyfriends, concerned mothers, federal representatives and almost everyone else in this, the first definite example of image-changing. The move was more than welcome, but ironically the film gained little acclaim.
STAY AWAY, JOE

to have a herd of cows and one bull, in the hope that he will become a successful cattle breeder. If it all works out, then the opportunistic congressman, due to his personal involvement in a public-spirited community scheme, will be one step closer to becoming Governor. At Joe's welcome-home party, where practically everyone gets drunk, the bull is inadvertently slaughtered by the inebriated Bronc, (L.Q. Jones) who has simply mistaken it for one of the cows. This act causes uproar and panic. Joe's exploits in attempting to secure a replacement bull form the basis for the remainder of the story. He carouses with several women, whether they are spoken-for or not, and sets his eyes on the teenage Mamie (Quentin Dean), daughter of the jealous Glenda (Joan Blondell). He fights with enemies and indeed with friends too, and incurs the wrath of Glenda, who makes several attempts to kill him. The film ends with a free-for-all fist fight and not with the customary romantic entanglement.

His womanizing in this film was far more adult, and it was certainly not before time. There were several references to more than just innocent kissing. Elvis was, at long last, growing up on screen. The irony is that *Stay Away, Joe* was the first Elvis Presley film to be denied a general release in the UK. It was granted a limited release in early 1969, but was not seen by the majority of general film-goers.

Since it constituted the first major change for Elvis regarding screen roles, this non-acceptance was a great disappointment. What was clearly wrong was the timing. If Elvis had switched to this role, or a similar adult role, around 1963 or 1964, instead of being swallowed up in glossy musicals, his future as a cinema performer would probably have been assured.

Alas, although aesthetically *Stay Away, Joe* was the correct career move, it was clearly made too late.

Live a Little, Love a Little

With the established formula now broken, Elvis proceeded to make films in a more adult vein. In March 1968 he began work on MGM's *Live a Little, Love a Little*, in which he played a top fashion photographer. Considered as something of a curiosity, due mainly to the strange happenings in the story including a weird dream sequence, the film moved along at a frantic pace.

On his final Elvis Presley film was director Norman Taurog. The producer, on his third successive Presley film, was Douglas Laurence. The screenplay was written by Michael A. Hoey (who scripted *Stay Away, Joe*) and Dan Greenburg, from Greenburg's own novel, the pretentiously titled *Kiss my Firm but Pliant Lips*.

The supporting cast again represented different generations. The female lead was taken by the vivacious Michelle Carey, whose performance as the seductive but scatterbrained Bernice was a shade over the top. Don Porter, as the liberated boss of a glamour magazine business was clearly a parody of *Playboy*'s Hugh Hefner.

Former vaudeville star Rudy Vallee, himself a successful musical performer, played Elvis's boss, a man obsessed with establishing an impeccable appearance in his employees. Elvis's own father Vernon Presley, was seen in a brief non-speaking part, in a photo session. Eleven years earlier, in Elvis's second film *Loving You*, Vernon and Elvis's mother Gladys could be seen sitting in the audience at the film's finale.

In the story, Elvis plays Greg Nolan, a successful photographer who has a chance meeting with the eccentric and possessive Bernice (Michelle Carey). She slips him a hallucinatory pill which knocks him out for days. Upon his return to work, he is immediately fired. After a brawl with his ex-employers, he connivingly engages in two full-time jobs for separate companies – with two bosses, namely Penlow (Rudy Vallee) and Lansdown (Don Porter). Bernice claims to have fallen for Greg, but another man, Harry (Dick Sargent), seems also to be forever in her life. Greg is extremely confused and attempts to dismiss the crazy girl from his life but she will not go away.

Despite obvious difficulties, Greg manages to maintain his two-pronged working existence until eventually his secret ploy is revealed.

Realizing that he is now in love with Bernice, he returns to her beach house where he informs her of his feelings.

For all that this vehicle and Elvis's previous one represented a stronger challenge, *Live a Little, Love a Little* still retained annoyingly childish ingredients. Detrimental to the overall production was Michelle Carey's over-playing of the psychologically unbalanced Bernice.

A big surprise was that Elvis shared a bed with Michelle Carey (albeit initially separated by a board), a scene hardly imaginable in any previous film. Of course nothing explicit was shown in this scene – Elvis Presley films were not quite ready for such radical changes.

Even the dialogue was at last more adult. Elvis actually got to say 'Dammit', which was, for him, tantamount to blasphemy in early 1968. In an early scene, referring to his employer, he asked a girl: 'How is the old sonofab ...?' That was as far as he got; but it was a relief to hear him using what is in effect everyday language.

Producer Douglas Laurence, who described Elvis as 'the biggest entertainer the world has ever known', had this to say in an on-set interview: 'Maybe this is sexy by Presley standards, but actually this is a kind of comedy. Elvis makes family pictures, and that's what this is.' Elvis himself said: 'No, it doesn't embarrass me to play a sexy scene.'

The lengthy fight sequence in the film was distinctly brutal. Playing the heavies were as ever, Red West, and with him this time his cousin Sonny West. Elvis, of course, emerged triumphant from this mêlée. As Red West succinctly put it: 'In all the films, I always ended up on my ass.'

Elvis was very believable as a fashion photographer, and it was indeed refreshing to see him in a meaningful and different part, not as a band leader or a race driver again.

Below: Twenty-eight film on and an adult role at last. He plays a fashion photographer employed by a glamour magazine.
Left: Elvis and Michelle Carey (pictured) share a bedroom scene together. Though not explicit in any way, such activity was unthinkable in previous films.
LIVE A LITTLE, LOVE A LITTLE

The music in the film, like the previous one, was brief – just four songs, and that included one over the credits. This was the mellifluous 'Wonderful World', which had been written by the British songwriting team of Doug Flett and Guy Fletcher. They later wrote another song that Elvis recorded, called 'The Fair's Moving on'. An excellent song called 'Edge of Reality' was featured in a dream sequence.

The single from the film consisted of the remaining two songs, namely 'A Little Less Conversation' and 'Almost in Love', which failed to make any impression on the charts.

Live a Little, Love a Little was released in the United States prior to Christmas 1968, but was never released in the UK. This was the first occasion this had occurred. It was a full ten years, in 1978, before the film even turned up on the 16mm catalogues, and it finally had its first UK television screening in 1986.

Despite minor problems, *Live a Little, Love a Little* was a good, well-produced film. The scenery was colourful and attractive, with much of it being shot around the Malibu Beach area. It was highly unfortunate that it was so readily dismissed by UK distributors.

Charro!

The year was 1968 when Elvis firmly transcended the light-hearted musical, and in the spring of that year it was announced that he was soon to begin work on a dramatic western called *Come Hell, Come Sundown*. More than ever before, this news was greatly welcomed.

At the end of June, Elvis taped the historic NBC-Singer sponsored television special at the Burbank studios in California. Just weeks later he was on location at Apache Junction, Arizona, working on the new western, now entitled *Charro!* for the National General Picture Corporation. This was to be the only occasion that Elvis would work for this film company, who were also responsible for a John Wayne western called *Big Jake* in 1971.

Most of the movie was shot around the Superstition mountains area of Arizona, and in fact the cast and crew stayed at the appropriately named Superstition Inn Motel, just outside Phoenix during the location shooting. A number of fans were fortunate enough to be photographed with Elvis off the set – an uncommon occurrence on other productions.

Interiors for the film were shot at the Sam Goldwyn studios in Hollywood.

Charro! was a novel by Harry Whittington. The credits of the film tell us that the story was by Frederic Louis Fox and also that the film was written, produced and directed by Charles Marquis Warren. It would seem that Warren was responsible for the story as seen on screen, and it is a pity. Very few people are capable of producing, directing *and* turning out a polished screenplay. A great deal of the dialogue was weak, inappropriate, and hopelessly clichéd.

Charles Marquis Warren was basically a television director, and it showed in the rather cramped approach. He had been involved in bringing the long-running 'Rawhide' television series for CBS onto the small screen and directed several of the early episodes.

The designed intention behind the whole *Charro!* project was laudable. Having allowed Elvis to change his image to a noticeable degree in his two previous films, this one was going to present an Elvis Presley hitherto unseen in the cinema.

For the first time ever, and in his twenty-ninth motion picture, Elvis Presley did not sing on screen. Throughout the entire film, he appears sombre and impassive. Few smiles, if any, ever cross his face.

Physically Elvis looked perfect for his portrayal of a tough gunfighter. With his lean frame, dirty clothes and rough beard, he appeared every inch to represent the type. The promotion for the film read 'A Different Kind of Role, A Different Kind of Man'. In comparison to previous form, it certainly lived up to that description.

The supporting cast was a mixed bag. Ina Balin provided the love interest, whilst the role of Elvis's antagonist was played by Victor French, whose acting was decidedly overwrought. An even more exaggerated performance was given by Solomon Sturges (son of film director John Sturges) as the demented younger brother of Victor French.

James Sikking, later to find TV fame in 'Hill Street Blues' played the role of an ex-Confederate gun expert. Paul Brinegar, 'Wishbone' in the 'Rawhide' series, also had a part in the film.

Both Ina Balin and Charles Marquis Warren were interviewed on the set, and spoke at length about the project.

Ms Balin said 'The picture is called *Charro!* which is Spanish for "proud cowboy". It stars Elvis Presley in his very first straight dramatic role [she was obviously unaware of *Flaming Star*, *King Creole* and others]. He does no singing, no dancing, and that was one of the things that intrigued me about this; because it is a western it's set in 1870.'

Speaking of Elvis's vastly different appearance she said: 'In fact many people didn't recognize him. I know one time he went for a weekend to Vegas and nobody recognized him! He said it was an incredible experience and they'd walk by him, saying "Is it or isn't it?" But for me it was a marvellous experience working with Elvis, because I think he is an instinctively fine actor, and I think that some day he is going to prove to the world that he is not only a fine performer, but a very excellent actor.'

Charles Marquis Warren had this to say:

Nothing today that happens can be quite equated with what happened back in the 1870s. All during the filming my thought was we are presenting a new Elvis Presley. I guess you could call it the ultimate surprise. In the first place, he is going to be totally different physically. When I first saw Elvis, he still had his little amount of baby fat on him. I said, 'Elvis you are going to be riding with a lot of tall thin cowboys,' and in two weeks, I think he took off twenty pounds. I think a lot of people would like to know his secret; I'd like to know! We put a beard on him for the first time.

Elvis plays something that he has never played before. He actually is an anti-hero. He is not the hero in the story. He is a man that perhaps the audience might have difficulty in identifying with – especially his fans. For God's sake, what is this? Elvis Presley? He's a bad, mean, tough, rugged man. He's got a beard. He does anything, even his own stunts, which surprised me.

We have both violence and nudity in this film. Inasmuch as he has played with girls before, and they surround him, almost engulf him, I think this is the first time that Elvis has ever come up against a stark naked woman in any of his films.

You run a risk whenever you try to change a man's image. Now, they changed Dean Martin's image, and got away with it. That's what we hope we can do with Elvis. I just hope that people will like him without his guitar, without his singing, without his millions of girls around him. He has always been surrounded by everybody. He is always the sweet good little boy that everybody loves [he could not have seen *Flaming Star* either], and will come out happily in the end. I think this is going to be different. Nobody likes him. Nobody trusts him. Everybody is afraid of him. I think this is kind of new and different for Elvis.

The story has Elvis as Jess Wade, lured to a Mexican border town by a false message from his former gang. Disarming him, they take him into the mountains where they show him the famed Victory Gun, a cannon enshrined from the Napoleonic Wars, which they have stolen from the Mexican people. After their escape, they led the Mexican government to believe that he, Jess, was in fact the perpetrator of this foul deed, and had sustained a neck wound during the course of this action. The gang then proceed to brand his neck, and then leave him in desolate territory, without a horse.

He recovers sufficiently, breaks a wild horse, and rides on to the town of Rio Seco, where he still has one or two friends, including the sheriff. When the sheriff dies in an attack launched from the stolen cannon, Jess reluctantly assumes the role of surrogate lawman.

Capturing the crazed younger brother, he takes him into the hills, and in the gunplay which ensues he disposes of the gang, except for the leader (Victor French). Jess then returns him, and the stolen gun, to the rightful authorities, where he can vindicate his good name.

The basic story, though hardly original, had an acceptable plot. The main weakness was in its construction and hackneyed lines. In one sequence, Elvis poised for gunplay, says to Victor French, 'Just make a move, that's all I ask. Just make a move.' This archaic utterance would even have sounded dated in an early 1950's B-western, let alone a late-sixties full-budget production.

For a 1968 revenge western, it was not nearly violent enough. Clint Eastwood's *Hang 'em High*, directed by Ted Post (coincidentally connected with 'Rawhide' again as respectively, star and occasional director), and made in the same year, was extremely violent. The storyline was almost identical: man is brutally beaten; left for dead; horribly scarred on neck; survives and recovers; becomes lawman, and sets out in pursuit of his enemies. The sense of retribution in *Hang 'em High* seemed justifiable, due to the fact that the main character was an innocent man, wrongfully set upon and therefore obsessed with wreaking revenge on all those who hanged him. *Charro!* lacked this motivation. Although Jess Wade did in fact kill off most of the gang who branded him in the end, it was almost by accident, and not through an obsessive desire for vengeance.

167

Menacing and always suspicious, Elvis is seen here
with James Sikking, later to find fame in television's
'Hill Street Blues'.

CHARRO!

An action rehearsal scene. Physically, Elvis was perfect for the western genre. This was to be the only film in which he did not sing a note.

CHARRO!

The publicity blurb for the film ran: 'On his neck he wore the brand of a killer, on his hip he wore vengeance.' Sadly, the content did not match this particular line of promotion.

Elvis himself was as disappointed as anyone that the end result was a toned-down routine horse opera. In Charlie Hodge's book *Me 'n' Elvis* he explained how Elvis approached the director and voiced his discontent over why much of the violence had been removed from the original script. Charles Marquis Warren informed him that the studio wanted it that way. Elvis obviously resigned himself to their decision. He said to Warren: 'They must want a milktoast western. I'll tell you what, Mr Warren. If that's all they want, let's just do the best we can, and take the money and run.'

It is easy to appreciate Elvis's bitterness concerning studio decisions. What is inconceivable is the fact that in attempting to change his image they even reneged on that issue.

Indeed, its violent content was minimal. Upon the film's release in the UK in 1971 (three years after it was made), the branding scene was dreadfully edited. The 16mm version was intact, and in this complete form was violently realistic. In being cut for the cinema and subsequent TV screenings, the film, because of this inept and foolish censorship decision, lost much of its impact. Compared to the graphic violence of a film like Sam Peckinpah's *Straw Dogs*, also released in 1971, it was extremely tame, even in its complete form.

An even more ludicrous example of censorship, was the fact that two different versions of *Charro!* played the circuit at the same time – one with the semi-nude scene intact, the other with this same scene missing. Ina Balin emerges nude from a bath and since it was filmed from behind, it could hardly have been considered explicit anyway.

The music consisted of just one song, 'Charro!', heard over the opening credits. The song, like Elvis's portrayal, was in sombre mood and fitted nicely with the film's theme. The song was the B side of a single in the United States and turned up on a budget album in 1970 in the UK.

The music score, used effectively throughout the film, was by Hugo Montenegro, famed for his 1968 number one version of 'The Good, the Bad and the Ugly'. This was originally done by Ennio Morricone for the cult spaghetti western directed by Sergio Leone.

The prospect of seeing Elvis as a macho gunman was not exactly what it should have been, mostly through studio ineptitude and a feeble script. Early on, as mentioned in *Elvis 'n' Me* by Charlie Hodge with Charles Goodman, Elvis expressed his own dissatisfaction: 'Mr Warren's been taking out all the good stuff, I can't figure out why. The fights, the gunplay – all the rough stuff. You know, I'm beginning to feel like this *Charro!* character. I can do him, if they'll quit messing up the script.'

One salutary fact, however, was that the vestiges of the musical romp era were very definitely buried, and Elvis had moved beyond the constraints of that period.

The Trouble with Girls

Maintaining the standard set in the previous year, Elvis's next film was the fourth in succession to be based on an original novel. In October 1968, Elvis was back at MGM studios working on his thirtieth motion picture, called *The Trouble with Girls*. Whilst the title was fairly appropriate for the story it suggested a light-hearted vehicle which basically it was not. The entire setting of the story was the travelling 'Chautauqua' Show, and with this prominence, should have been retained as the title from the novel – *Chautauqua*, written by Day Keene and Dwight Babcock. On almost all the promotional material, the film is called *The Trouble with Girls (And How to Get into it)*. The sub-title, however, does not seem to appear on any actual prints of the film.

The director was Peter Tewksbury, who had also directed *Stay Away, Joe*. The producer was Lester Welch and the screenplay was written by Arnold and Lois Peyser.

Elvis had healthy support from his co-stars. The attractive Marlyn Mason was a bright and breezy female lead, and likewise Sheree North, an experienced actress, gave an admirable performance as a dissolute mother attempting to secure a future as an entertainer for her young daughter. Dabney Coleman played the local storekeeper. His infidelity with Sheree North was the catalyst for his eventual murder in the story. Coleman went on to a certain measure of success in, among others, two films with Jane Fonda, *Nine to Five* and *On Golden Pond*. Veteran actor Edward Andrews, as Elvis's right-hand man, was very engaging with his whimsical asides.

Appearing in cameo roles, and perhaps a most unusual choice for an Elvis Presley vehicle, were Vincent Price and John Carradine – both more familiar in horror films.

In the story, Elvis is cast as Walter Hale, manager of the travelling Chautauqua show, a 'canvas college', so named because of its blend of education with entertainment. The show comes to Radford Center, Iowa, and it is there that the

172

'trouble' of the title begins. Constant negotiation problems with the militant Charlene (Marlyn Mason), forever quoting union regulations, are a threat to Hale's tranquility. Nita Bix (Sheree North) tries desperately to have her young daughter auditioned as an entertainer, whilst she herself is having a clandestine affair with Wilby (Dabney Coleman), the local storekeeper. Another local girl, Betty Smith (Nicole Jaffe) is infatuated by the dashing manager, and seeks employment with the show.

Hale's cynical sidekick, Johnny Anthony (Edward Andrews) frequently reminds him that he is unlikely to cope with the mounting pressures put on the show. The affable Hale remains surprisingly unruffled at all this. A murder is committed in the area, casting a stigma on the Chautauqua. One of the staff, Clarence (Anthony Teague) is arrested, and Hale attempts to solve the crime himself, believing his employee to be innocent. Meanwhile, audiences are being held spellbound by the teachings of two prominent figures in the show, Mr Morality (Vincent Price) and Mr Drewcolt (John Carradine).

Following several leads, Hale's theatrical denouement proves the innocence of the wrongly accused. The Chautauqua has regained its respectability whilst Hale and Charlene see each other in a different light.

This was another period film for Elvis, and the flavour of the 1920s was captured admirably. The backgrounds and sets displayed what was an obviously well-planned reconstruction. The only factor possibly at odds with the era was Elvis's physical appearance. Where almost all the actors had short haircuts and staid clothes, Elvis, for most of the film, wore a striking white suit and hat, and had exceptionally long sideburns. But even if he was at odds with the period, he looked terrific physically, and was very much the focal point when on screen.

There was a bone of contention for Elvis Presley fans regarding his time on screen. Much of the plot took place without Elvis in camera and complaints were lodged that his part was more of a guest appearance. In the UK this did seem more of a point since, when the film was released in late

Elvis, sartorially resplendent as the cigar-smoking manager of a 1920s travelling tent show. The atmosphere of the period was captured remarkably well.
THE TROUBLE WITH GIRLS

1969, it had been mercilessly and inexplicably hacked from 104 to seventy-nine minutes. Twenty-five minutes is an awful lot of film to remove from a feature and still hope to retain the main plot essentials in the remnants. As it was, the shortened version made little sense, and would probably have been better left unreleased than to have been issued in this truncated form.

That same 1969 release was the first official B-feature categorizing of an Elvis Presley film; it ran second to a

174

forgettable fantasy adventure film. Such was the popularity, or rather the lack of it, of Elvis's films at that time.

In his three previous films, all contributing to his 'period of change' image, Elvis's sexuality was more evident. From seeing him in bed with a woman in *Live a Little, Love a Little* to viewing a naked woman emerging from a bath in *Charro!*, *The Trouble with Girls* presented him as, if not exactly lascivious, charmingly seductive.

On several occasions, Elvis's eye contact with Marlyn Mason seemed to be challenging her to a form of mating ritual. In one quiet scene, Elvis is seen to be sensuously massaging her shoulders, and openly suggests that perhaps they could continue their discourse in bed. Naturally, this scene formed part of the removed footage in the UK version. Perhaps MGM thought that Elvis Presley's British support would be flabbergasted to hear him utter such terribly 'suggestive' words. The strange part was that even in the complete version we never got to hear Marlyn Mason's answer.

Much of the film shows Elvis smoking cigars, a trait not really common in his screen appearances, although in his private life it seemed to be a fairly regular habit.

Elvis's performance was very smooth and professional. As the manager in a very responsible position, he was totally believable. His resolute calm amidst escalating hostilities was highly engaging and added much to the story's atmosphere.

As a change of direction, *The Trouble with Girls* was commendable. It was rather sad, however, that it turned out to be Elvis's penultimate acting role.

The opening sequence as the show arrives in a new town. The film's impact was almost totally destroyed upon its release in the UK when an unbelievable twenty-five minutes was excised from the original running time. THE TROUBLE WITH GIRLS

Change of Habit

January of 1969 saw Elvis back in the recording studios of Memphis for the first time since the 1950s to cut tracks for what was arguably his best post-army recording work. Following this, Elvis signed a contract to appear for one month (the following August) at the newly built International Hotel in Las Vegas, for what turned out to be a triumphant return to live stage appearances.

Sandwiched in between this, Elvis made his final scripted film, *Change of Habit* for Universal pictures. Shooting commenced in March, and although the setting was the ghettos of New York, the filming all took place in Los Angeles.

The director was William Graham, a man noted more for his work in television films. The producer on this occasion was Joe Connelly. The screenplay was written by James Lee, S.S. Schweitzer and Eric Bercovici, from a story by John Joseph and Richard Morris. With so many people involved, the finished script could have been visibly disjointed, but it was, in fact, a well-constructed plot, much in line with current times. The film took a sympathetic look at contemporary issues, like urban deprivation, squalor, racism and its associated violence.

Elvis's co-stars proved to be an efficient cast. Mary Tyler Moore had the main female lead as Sister Michelle, for whom Elvis (as John Carpenter) has a growing attraction, not realizing her vocation. Barbara McNair, as Sister Irene, was the black member of the trio, more capable of identifying with the local people. The third member, Sister Barbara, was played by Jane Elliot, whose character was resolutely idealistic.

Two faces familiar from Elvis's earlier *Kid Galahad* film, namely Edward Asner (of later 'Lou Grant' fame) and Robert Emhardt, played respectively a police lieutenant and a loanshark operator.

In the story, Elvis (John Carpenter) plays a young, caring doctor operating a free clinic with limited resources in the heart of a down-town ghetto. The local community consists mainly of blacks and Puerto Ricans who, like most ethnic minorities experience difficulty integrating with the host community. The result of this, of course, is frequent outbursts of violence and people living in constant fear.

Into this complex situation come three crusading nuns, who are working on a project instigated by the Catholic Action Committee. As part of an experiment, they dispense with their nun's clothing and seek employment as nurses (they are all qualified in this field). No one except the doctrinaire local priest, is aware of their true identity.

Dr Carpenter is reluctant to employ the assistance of the three ladies but he does relent, and they, in turn, prove to be a worthwhile appointment. During the course of their time at the clinic, the doctor is drawn to Michelle, who coldly rebuffs his advances. He fails to understand her aloofness, whilst she prays for divine answers to the predicament.

Among the many difficult cases they have to contend with are heroin users, a young autistic girl and an unstable young man with serious domestic problems. Apart from the medical inadequacies, the community is deprived financially, and many people in their desperation turn to the loansharks in the area. Sister Irene, in an effort to rout them, deliberately involves herself in this dangerous fraternity.

The nuns eventually have to reveal their true identity and the doctor angrily announces his disappointment that he has been seriously misled.

The story ends with Dr Carpenter singing at a mass where the nuns are present, and Sister Michelle trying to decide between love for him or love for God. The answer to her dilemma is still unclear by the close of the credits. The audience can make up its own mind as to her decision.

Photoplay film magazine stated that there was a current trend for films involving nuns, quoting *Change of Habit* and another Universal film being made around the same time, the Don Siegel western *Two Mules for Sister Sara*, starring Clint Eastwood and Shirley Maclaine.

During production, a report from Hollywood, by one Bertil Unger, appeared in the Glasgow *Evening Times* and ran like this:

Rock 'n' Roll singers come and go, but the one who really started it all still lingers on. The big daddy of them all, Elvis Aaron Presley – who, of course, isn't using the name Aaron much any more – is as big a name today as he was over a dozen years ago when he was called 'The Pelvis'.

Either he should be shot on sight for starting the whole noise, or revered like a god. And I'm not for shooting him.

He has always followed the times, and had smart advice from his mentor, Colonel Parker. He quit mumbling his songs; started singing ballads when he returned from his military service; stayed out of television until recently (in case of over-exposure); stuck to his films, which all are making money in spite of the bad scripts; and remained a clean-cut fellow, and the most polite man in Hollywood.

He still doesn't smoke, or drink anything stronger than milk, and I'm sure he never has taken any drug stronger than aspirin.

He *is* married though – even a father!

He now has the image of something between Dudley Do-right of the mounties and Prince Valiant, and I don't believe he ever uses naughty words.

How can be possibly surpass himself any more?

Well, while stars like Rex Harrison and Richard Burton play fags in drag in *The Staircase*, Elvis is now turning around and going dramatic.

In his current Universal picture, *Change of Habit*, a poignant drama, he plays a doctor, who forms a strong affectionate friendship with a nun.

And it is all done without any songs. Not a single twang on a guitar.

A long step from the days when his hips went berserk while he sang 'Hound Dog' or 'Jailhouse Rock' in the mid fifties.

But maybe Harrison and Burton can take over where he left off?

After all, as we know, they both sing too.

This stunningly simplistic yet descriptive report was ironically mocked some years later, in the flood of books denouncing Elvis as a licentious, foul-mouthed drug abuser.

Right: The film's climax: Elvis sings with a crowd gathered in chapel. The music was brief but appropriate. *Below*: The transition into 1970s 'social issues' drama. Elvis plays a young doctor helping ethnic minorities in a deprived area of New York. The film captures the essence of contemporary social problems in its account of racial tension, squalor and dangerous loanshark operators. Mary Tyler Moore plays a nun with whom the doctor becomes involved.
CHANGE OF HABIT

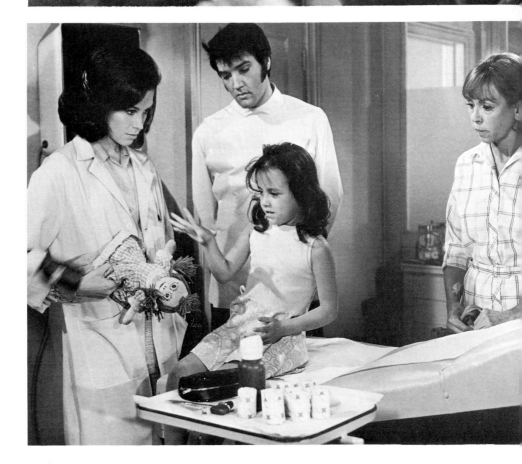

His image in 1969 was, to all intents and purposes, faultless.

The music in the film, consisting of only four songs, was appropriately placed. From the title song over the opening credits, to the semi-rock 'Rubberneckin' with Elvis on guitar; to the carnival-like 'Have a Happy' (still sung to a child, but somehow more acceptably); to the closing 'Let us Pray' sung in the chapel, the songs provided a lively atmosphere. Elvis also played a very bluesy version of 'Lawdy Miss Clawdy' on piano, with no vocals.

There was no single release from the film, but 'Rubberneckin'' did emerge as the B-side of Elvis's 1970 'Don't Cry Daddy' single. The other three songs appeared hidden away on budget albums.

Change of Habit was released in the States in January 1970, and provided cinema-goers with a view of Elvis Presley as yet unseen on the screen. This was a smooth and highly efficient transition into the film world of the 1970s.

Despite the film's obvious superiority it was not released in the UK. Over two years after its production, in August 1971, the BBC presented a première showing as part of a short Elvis Presley season. The reviews were almost all complimentary and the question most prominent among those same reviews was: 'Why was this film denied full cinema distribution?' Why indeed? Compared to something like *Clambake*, made only two years before, *Change of Habit* was like a breath of fresh air. This sentiment was reiterated by several reviewers, who, upon seeing the film realized the absurdity of its withdrawal from cinemas.

The night after the television screening, Jim Hewitson of the Glasgow *Evening Times* commented thus:

It's not often we get the première of a film in our own front rooms, but last night the good old BBC surpassed themselves with positively the first showing on this side of the Atlantic of the Elvis Presley film *Change of Habit*.

It really was worth watching. Elvis kept the singing to a minimum, and showed us that he is an actor of some merit.

In a *West Side Story* setting, Elvis played a young doctor trying cheerfully to live with the race problems around him. When three nuns appear on the scene, having dispensed with their black habits for two months to 'get among the people', the fun really starts.

Mary Tyler Moore, as one of the nuns, almost, I repeat almost, fell in love with the doctor.
There was humour, social comment, singing and dancing.
But perhaps the most impressive scene was Elvis, aided by the nuns, helping to set an autistic child on the road to recovery.

It's seldom that the BBC come up with a film that you can truly say you enjoyed. This just happened to be one of the best.

Superlative praise indeed. A more unusual, though still commendatory view came from the film reviewer Philip Jenkinson, who said: 'Presley's recent excursions in the movies have either been totally pop (*That's the Way it Is*) or dramatic pieces like this one. I'm a little mystified that he should choose to go straight when he is still the undisputed king of rock. But he makes a good job of his part and the only people likely to be disappointed are the fans old or nostalgic enough to pine for the days of *Jailhouse Rock* and *GI Blues*.

Jenkinson is mystified as to why Elvis should 'choose to go straight' – more mystifying is the basis for this comment, which questioned Elvis's right to attempt more dramatic, meaningful films. Such was the paradox of Elvis Presley as a screen performer. For years he had endured constant criticism for his lightweight films and was repeatedly advised by critics to move into a more dramatic area. When he did eventually accede to this 'advice', what happened? His new career decisions then became a subject of debate. It was very clear that Elvis Presley could never satisfy his critics, no matter how laudable his attempts to diversify.

Change of Habit was a praiseworthy project, enhancing Elvis's image as an adult actor: the film was entertaining, well acted, and had a message to put across. With scenes including attempted rape, the dangers of moneylending and the distress of heroin addicts, this proved a radical transformation of the stereotypical 'Elvis Presley film'.

What is hugely regrettable, is that Elvis at thirty-four years of age and looking physically better on screen than ever before, thus concluded his acting career forever. Thirty-one acting roles by the age of thirty-four may seem like an over-abundance, but there was clearly much scope for him to continue as a film performer, though perhaps not so prolifically.

His progress into the dramatic arena was right; his timing was not.

Again, the much-discussed subject of Elvis's disaffection with his film career did not manifest itself in this production. His performance, in fact, gave more credence to his own desire to work in similarly dramatic vehicles.

Alas, in his physical prime and with potentially a whole new career ahead of him, *Change of Habit* marked Elvis Presley's final acting role. The waste of talent was horrendous. Although many further offers came his way he would never again appear in a scripted film.

6 *Documentary Elvis: A New Concept (1970–72)*

This is the best film I have ever made.
Elvis Presley referring to MGM's Elvis – That's the Way it is.

Elvis – That's the Way it is

After Elvis's enormously successful return to the stage in the summer of 1969, following an eight-year break from public appearances, he played the International Hotel in Las Vegas for a further season in January 1970. Immediately after this he performed six concerts at the huge Astrodome in Houston, Texas. His third season in Las Vegas was then announced. It would again begin in August, and would be called 'Elvis's Summer Festival'. Once the contracts were in order, the media exposure began.

The suggestion of filming Elvis's Las Vegas stage act, thereby presenting him 'in cabaret' to a truly worldwide audience, was to become the MGM documentary *Elvis – That's the Way it is* – his thirty-second film.

Having played two seasons at the International Hotel, Elvis was by now more confident and relaxed. His approach and reactions to cameras being around him in concert would be less disconcerting, due to his familiarity with the surroundings and, especially, the audience.

The film was tentatively entitled *Elvis*, and apart from much footage of his stage act, the filming of rehearsals, backstage frolics fan interviews and other associated Elvis happenings would also take place. This was all done in an effort to encapsulate the Elvis Presley legend – to show to the world the enormity of his talent, his power, his following.

Musical documentaries were not exactly an innovative trend at that time. Prior to this project there had been the 1968 film, *Johnny Cash – the Man, his World, his Music*, and director and consummate film-maker D.A. Pennebaker had brought to the cinema *Don't Look Back*, a 1967 film of a Bob Dylan tour, and *Monterey Pop* (1968). There were other films featuring performers in the pop/rock music field, but most of these documentaries could only be seen in arts cinemas. Few were given full promotion due to the limitations of the subject matter. *Elvis – That's the Way it is*, on the other hand, enjoyed world-wide distribution and was handled as a fully commercial property. MGM, which was presenting a very different type of Elvis Presley film to its twelve previous vehicles, obviously decided that potentially they had an enormous hit movie, so why not give it the full treatment?

Director Denis Sanders oversees camera set-ups inside the International Hotel in Las Vegas.
ELVIS, THAT'S THE WAY IT IS

The man assigned as director for the project was Denis Sanders, who had already won two Academy Awards as a documentary film-maker for *A Time out for War* and *Czechoslovakia 1968*. His own musical interests lay in jazz, of which he was an early devotee. He confessed to have known little of Elvis Presley, but was openly enthusiastic about his attempt to present a graphic account of the Elvis phenomenon.

The inclusion of interviews with fans was Sanders' own idea, because in his view, the audience was every bit as important as the entertainer. His own assessment of the film's motivation was this: 'In a way, it's a film by one professional about another professional in another field. So I have no interest, really, in his personal life. I really don't. My interest is solely in Elvis as a performer ... as a multi-talented performer, and as a musician.'

Of Elvis himself he stated: 'I think he's fantastic. I knew he was fanastic the very first time I saw him in rehearsal. I knew where he was. From then on I knew what I wanted to go after. He's got what Brando had at that perfect moment in his career where you couldn't anticipate Brando as an actor. That's what Presley has. The audience can't anticipate him.'

The film, already graced with Sanders' expertise, was further enhanced by the stunning camera work of the talented cinematographer Lucien Ballard, who had photographed, amongst other things, the celebrated Stanley Kubrick film *The Killing* (1956); several Sam Peckinpah westerns, including *The Wild Bunch* (one of the first films to feature explicit slow-motion violence); and, again in the western vein, on several John Wayne films, including the Oscar-winning *True Grit*. Through the lens of Ballard's camera, Elvis Presley was seen as a man of many guises: the joker, clowning with his musicians in the studios; the unsure artist, going over and over song lyrics even when he should have been relaxing backstage, and needing reassurance from his colleagues; the professional showman, proving his undeniable talent in a breathtaking show, performed to a capacity audience.

Elvis did not appear to be inhibited by cameras and recording apparatus during his stage performances. Many years spent around such equipment no doubt accounted for this.
ELVIS, THAT'S THE WAY IT IS

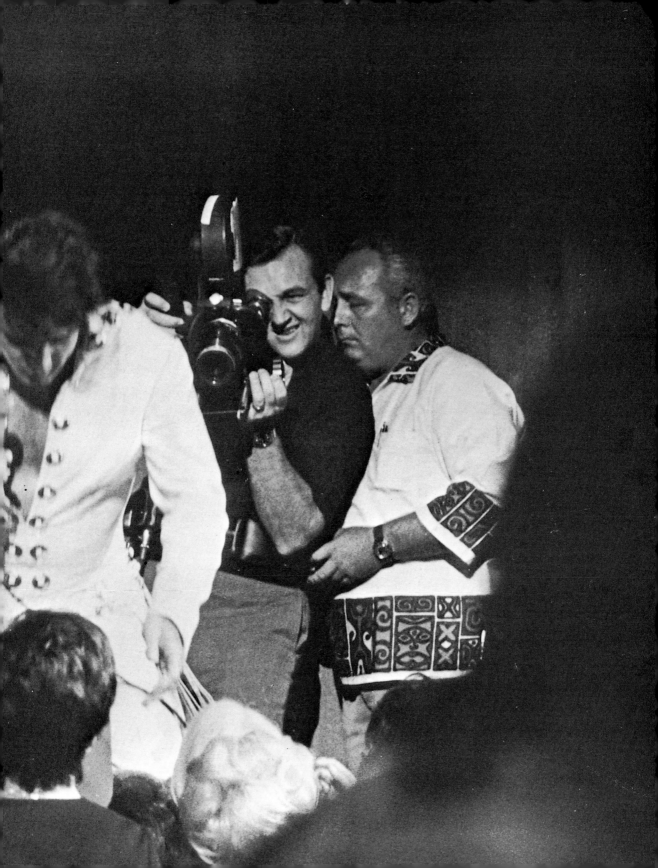

The excitement generated by the news of the documentary was evidenced in an August 1970 edition of the *Hollywood Reporter*, which stated:

Las Vegas – the MGM crew headed by director Denis Sanders, here to film Elvis Presley's appearance at the International Hotel, reports that as a result of his appearance: nine couples have named their children Elvis; four young men are making every attempt to look like the star; five fans over 80 will attend every show through Labor Day; and 31 fans will attend both shows a night; three camper vans are covered with pictures of Elvis; and fans from 32 states and 16 countries are gathered here just for the event.

The film opens with a gyrating Elvis seen through a strobe light, performing a medley of 'Mystery Train' and 'Tiger Man'. This sequence was filmed at a concert in Phoenix, Arizona in September 1970, representing Elvis's first tour concert since his stage return. The remainder of the film was shot in Las Vegas, with rehearsal scenes also filmed at MGM's Culver City studios. The many rehearsal scenes shown were obviously played up for the cameras, but they do give a fascinating insight into just what takes place in a recording studio – an area normally considered sacrosanct, and which the general public knows little about. That same year, the final Beatles film *Let it Be*, also revealed the inner workings of the recording studio technique.

The build-up to the actual concert via interviews with fans, hotel staff, Las Vegas citizens, and celebrities instils a mounting excitement in the viewer – almost as if he or she were at the concert, eagerly anticipating the main event.

When the lights go down and all is quiet, Elvis's dramatic entrance on stage is a sight to behold. To thunderous applause he launches straight into his first ever recording, 'That's Alright Mama'. This was performed by a confident Elvis, complete with an unamplified, and therefore symbolic, guitar!

The songs which follow range from older hits to contemporary songs like 'Bridge over Troubled Water' and 'You've Lost that Loving Feeling'. These two songs were given powerhouse treatment, each reaching a staggering climax. 'Polk Salad Annie' and 'Suspicious Minds' were also songs that, with the visual pyrotechnics, made for absorbing viewing.

The climactic 'Can't Help Falling in Love' closes the concert and the film. The audience rises for a lengthy standing ovation – a tribute to this man who held them spellbound, and who, in their eyes, unquestionably deserves this undivided attention. In freeze-frame, Elvis Presley offers his salute.

The human side of Elvis away from 'formula' characterizations is displayed in the documentary on two occasions when he commits the cardinal sin (for him that is) of being heard to swear. On the first occasion when he receives a shock from a faulty microphone, he says: 'Goddamit! ... Sonofabitch!'. The second instance is when he is having further microphone problems, only this time on stage. He lifts four different microphones, turns to the band and says: 'You can't lose with four of these bastards, man!' Both occasions were off-microphone but still audible and had they been part of the normal sound level no doubt the film would not have been granted a U certificate by the Board of Censors.

Elvis was as excited as everyone over the project. He declared that it was the best film that he had ever made. The euphoria over his return to stage appearances was of course responsible for his statement, although the film could never really be compared to the likes of *King Creole* or *Wild in the Country*, since the documentary is an entirely different type of cinema.

Disappointments with the production were centred on the over-use of fan interviews, which though initially interesting, tended eventually to fragment the basic structure. Likewise the inclusion of a sequence on stage where Elvis says, 'Have we got "The Wonder of You" on the chart over there?' and then to go on and not present the song, showed a lack of attention regarding continuity flow.

In the UK the film was given a prestigious première at the Royal Festival Hall in London in April 1971, prior to its general release a few weeks later.

Elvis – That's the Way it is presented a glowing Elvis Presley, now thirty-five years old and immensely enjoying his return to his first love – being on stage and performing to a live audience. His charismatic presence excited everyone, and it was clear that the rapport he had with an audience was something he could never achieve on a film set.

The film enjoyed commercial success to such a degree that MGM did not wait too long to announce a similar follow-up project.

Elvis on Tour

In early 1972 MGM announced that they were about to embark on a new project for Elvis Presley. The film would be built around his upcoming fifteen-city tour which was to begin in Buffalo, New York in April. It was to be called 'Standing Room Only' to emphasize the concert footage, but was wisely changed by the end of production to *Elvis on Tour* – a simple title, brief but descriptive.

The idea of presenting Elvis removed from Las Vegas trappings and instead working to a hectic schedule 'on the road' was highly commendable and proved educational to those people who were genuinely interested in seeing first-hand the formidable work attached to concert tour arrangements. The finished film had a breathless atmosphere, displaying clearly that the music business was not an arena of peace and tranquillity, but one where only diligent dedicated people could survive.

The assignment was zealously pursued by producer/ directors Pierre Adidge and Robert Abel – two men who took their subject most seriously. Together they had just completed another music documentary, *Mad Dogs and Englishmen*, a film featuring British singer Joe Cocker. Abel had expressed his disappointment with *Elvis – That's the Way it is*, claiming that it had told people very little about Elvis Presley the man. That film had centred exclusively on Elvis as an entertainer, and Abel felt that their production would give a clearer insight into the thoughts and motivations of a musical legend. In all fairness to Denis Sanders and his earlier documentary, he had made it abundantly clear that Elvis's private life was of no interest to him as a film-maker and that his sole intention was to present a cinematic portrait of Elvis Presley in what he did best – entertaining the public.

Adidge and Abel obviously saw a need for giving cinema-goers another view of Elvis Presley, while still retaining that essential ingredient of his appeal, his contribution to music. The eager film-makers' initial meeting with Elvis and Colonel Parker was in February 1972, backstage at the Hilton Hotel in Las Vegas. After their discussion of intended tactics, Adidge and Abel left without receiving a firm commitment on the project. Colonel Parker, always cautious, did not grant them his full approval until some time later, after they had in fact shot a considerable amount of footage. Once they were given the green light, their zeal for the film became all but obsessive.

In stylish *cinéma vérité* form, *Elvis on Tour* represented far more than just a simple display of Elvis Presley's seventies image. The icon, and its origins, was to a degree analysed. The resultant findings could be considered a prime example of the American Dream. Elvis Presley *was* the poor-boy-made-good – certainly neither the original nor the definitive case, but one with which millions of American people could easily identify. Elvis himself at no time ever attempted to analyse or question his phenomenal career. When asked for his own views, he consistently stated that he was 'just lucky'.

Through the media of documentary film, the reasons for Elvis Presley's rise to fame became that much clearer. With the use of old family photographs, kinescopes from early television shows and a relaxed-sounding Elvis providing his own voice-overs, a total rather than fragmented picture of the man emerged. The film-makers had persuaded Elvis to sit and reminisce about the early days, his feelings about music, his family and so on, and ended up with an exclusive two-hour taped interview. In total, only a few minutes of this material is actually heard on the soundtrack.

Similarly, as with the famous saying about film 'ending up on the cutting-room floor', much of *Elvis on Tour* met the same end. Although around fifty hours of film was shot during production, the finished film ran for only 93 minutes. That left an awful lot of Elvis Presley's life lying on a shelf somewhere.

The sequence in the film showing a montage of photographs spanning Elvis's life, which neatly develops into an early monochrome television appearance, was handled by Martin Scorsese, now an enormously successful film director with many excellent films to his credit. (Among these were *Taxi Driver* (1976), *The Colour of Money* (1986), and in 1978 *The Last Waltz* – a filmed account of the last stage appearance by The Band.)

For *Elvis on Tour*, Scorsese was credited as 'Montage Supervisor'. In the book, *The Movie Brats* by Michael Pye and Lynda Miles, it is stated that Scorsese has dissociated himself from the film. Is this again reaction to the ugly stigma of having known to be associated with Elvis Presley films? The ironic aspect of this action is that *Elvis on Tour* won a Golden Globe Award as Best Documentary Film of 1972 – the only Presley film to ever achieve such a distinction.

Displaying a trend for experimentation, as did most independent films, almost all of *Elvis on Tour* is represented in multiple image. This split-screen technique could be extremely beneficial to a production, and in fact a small measure of this format was witnessed in *Elvis – That's the Way it is*, two years earlier. In allowing practically the entire film to be seen in this way the decision could be considered as innovative, even effective, but it is also at times confusing. Perhaps if the ratio had been fifty-fifty, it would not have been so ultimately distracting.

Slow-motion filming is also used to considerable effect, especially in the opening 'Johnny B. Goode' sequence. The promotion for the film claimed it as 'The Magic and Excitement of Elvis Live in Concert', and from its energetic opening to its sedate fadeout, the production maintains this promotional boast.

The choice of music was interesting and varied. One disappointment was the fact that the film could have presented different songs, instead of including 'repeats' from the previous documentary, 'Polk Salad Annie' and 'Bridge over Troubled Water' are shown in full, as had been the case in *Elvis – That's the Way it is*, whereas a previously unfilmed song like 'Until it's Time for You to Go' is only seen in truncated form – a mere few lines. More unusual songs should have been chosen, variety being of paramount importance.

Top left: An emotional outpouring on stage during his hectic multi-city tour. Elvis's concerts were always sold out. *Bottom left:* Producer-directors Pierre Adidge and Robert Abel discuss details with a colleague. Beside them is a wealth of film footage only ninety-three minutes of which were used for the final film. *Right:* Proudly displaying the gold belt he had been awarded the previous year by the International Hotel in Las Vegas for the World's Championship Attendance Record.
ELVIS ON TOUR

The on-stage repertoire is nevertheless exciting. Elvis's strong rendition of contemporary songs such as 'Proud Mary' and 'Never Been to Spain' demand keen attention. Likewise, 'I Got a Woman' and 'Lawdy Miss Clawdy' show Elvis at his charismatic best. The haunting and beautifully orchestrated 'An American Trilogy' is a powerhouse performance and a captivating screen experience.

Elvis's love of gospel music is never better displayed than when he sincerely requests the audience to be silent while the Stamps Quartet sing (without musical accompaniment) the telling 'Sweet Sweet Spirit'. The cameras were allowed to dwell on Elvis's face while the song was being performed, and it appears to be far more of a joyous experience for him than it is for the gathered crowd. Off-stage, in a much more relaxed situation Elvis along with J.D. Sumner and the Stamps, is seen happily engaged in a gospel music singing session.

A recording-studio session is witnessed once again, this time taken from the March 1972 visit to the RCA Studios in Hollywood. The song in question is 'Separate Ways', which was issued as a single backed with 'Always on my Mind' later that same year.

The haste of concert tour arrangements is shown in a montage of trips between cars, airports, hotels and various venues. One particular sequence depicts Elvis being hurriedly escorted to his limousine immediately following his departure from the stage, and with the astounding volume of fans, reporters, police officers and photographers all jostling for a better vantage point, the scene comes over as extremely frightening – a harrowing experience for the security team on each occasion. The safety aspect of the concerts came very much into question.

The nostalgic look at Elvis's early career, firstly through photographs and then the excerpts from the 1956 'Ed Sullivan Show', made for interesting comparisons. The change in Elvis, physically, sartorially and artistically, was quite stunning. The raw and primitive country boy was now an accomplished, professional and acutely confident stage performer. At the age of 37, Elvis had been a musical legend for almost half of his life. His prominence was not something that he had had to work at. In fact he had eschewed many forms of promotional publicity in the 1950s. He was clearly possessed of a talent which sold itself. In *Elvis on Tour*, his undeniable charisma is very evident, even infectious.

The film trailer for *Elvis on Tour* began with the statement: 'MGM presents a different kind of motion picture.' These words were now a prominent feature of Elvis Presley's recent cinematic ventures. The promotion for *Charro!* had declared 'A Different Kind of Role, A Different Kind of Man', and the US film trailer for *Change of Habit* announced 'A Different Kind of Elvis Presley'. Someone was taking this attempt at image-change very seriously. *Elvis on Tour* could not really be compared with the first documentary as the motivation behind each project was distinctly different.

Despite announcements and rumours of future projects for the cinema, this film remained Elvis's final one. After thirty-three feature films, he terminated his association with the medium forever. The last frames of *Elvis on Tour* show a close-up of Elvis Presley travelling in a limousine, deep in thought: it stops in freeze-frame. This was to represent his final appearance on a cinema screen.

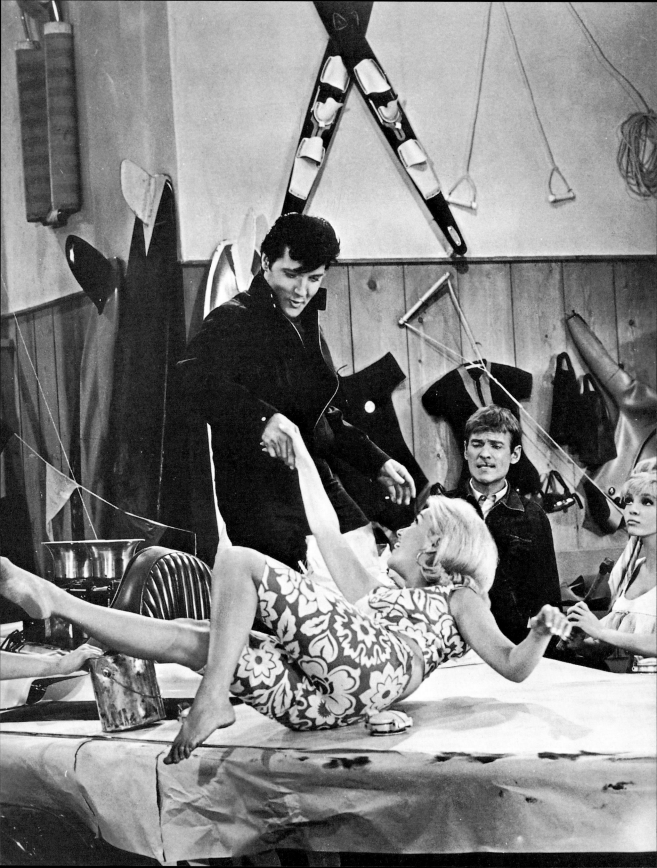

7 An Appraisal

*The trouble was, Hollywood just had the wrong image of me –
and there was nothing I could do about it.*

Elvis Presley on film

Why was Elvis Presley's Hollywood career so greatly maligned? Was it in fact the non-success everyone claimed? The box-office results tell us different: every film he starred in made money. Some made a great deal of money.

Elvis's superior films were among his first few and his last few. It was the films in-between that were the real problem and the main focus of harsh criticism and virtual dismissal by the doyens of cinema taste.

What made a man like Elvis Presley accept a script like *Harum Scarum* or *Clambake*? Either he was by that time totally indifferent to what was offered or he was one of the poorest judges of material in the film business. If it was the latter, then he was not alone because, as already mentioned, many notable leading players have appeared in monumental disasters.

The answer undoubtedly lies in the former theory. At the height of his film-making, he completed three features a year. It would be almost impossible to (a) be visibly enthusiastic about such frequency and (b) produce a high quality output in such a limited period. What Elvis should have done was confine himself to only one film per year – carefully selecting a script that had obvious quality. The reason that this did not happen was pure greed and nothing else. Colonel Parker was accustomed to the enormous income that was garnered from just one film and strived to maintain,

Elvis and friends in beach party mood.
CLAMBAKE

201

if not improve upon, that earning potential. He expedited each new contract with a zealous, almost obsessive approach.

Elvis himself was not a totally innocent party. He too was used to a large income. His problem was that he was such a great benefactor to the many people around him that he was spending money every bit as fast as he was earning it. The countless examples of his overwhelming generosity to family, friends and even total strangers are simply astounding. On a mere whim, he would go on an enormous spending spree, freely dispensing lavish gifts to those he considered deserving. There are numerous tales of people remarking to him that they admired a particular piece of expensive jewellery he was wearing, and Elvis would, without hesitation, remove the item in question and give it to the admirer.

He *needed* a consistently high income to satisfy his outrageous expenditure and it came to him in the form of movies. Certainly he also earned large sums of money from his recordings, but the success of a particular record was less assured. With his films it was different: this area guaranteed a good income. The Colonel's price for any film starring Elvis was $1 million plus fifty per cent of the profit. In the 1960s this was a staggering sum, and one has to admire Colonel Parker for his business acumen in securing such contracts. Even if a film did flop (which they invariably did not) both Elvis and Colonel Parker still received a sizeable amount – that being the obligatory $1 million.

Speaking of the disparity between Elvis's financial and creative desires on the BBC radio broadcast 'The Elvis Enigma' in January 1989, Tom Jones said:

> He wanted to be a serious actor. He used to study Marlon Brando pictures, James Dean, you know, method acting ... he wanted to be that kind of actor. But Colonel Tom Parker said, I mean I heard him say it myself. He said this: 'People ask me, do you like this script for Elvis?' He said, 'I don't even want to read the script. If you can pay a million dollars, Elvis will do the movie. I don't care if it's about Mickey Mouse!' So, as far as

Elvis was concerned he was listening to his manager's advice and that advice was money. If they can give us the money, you do the movie.

And another thing Parker told me: there was a movie offered to Elvis, and it was said that if he did this role, it looked like an Oscar nomination, but there was no money involved. So Parker laughingly told me, 'I said to these people. Give me a million dollars. Elvis will do the movie. If he gets the Oscar, I'll give you the million back.' And he thought that was a wonderful idea, but he would not let Elvis do it without the million dollars, even if there was the possibility of an Oscar. So Elvis had no chance of making a serious movie, because he wasn't allowed to.

Elvis was guilty of not attempting to change the situation regarding choice of script. When he eventually did, the move was timed far too late. He was clearly content to remain on the bandwagon, from a financial point of view. Perhaps if he had had better advisors in this area, his generosity would have been more controlled. The fact that he so readily parted with enormous sums of money for others less fortunate was in itself admirable. More difficult to accept is why he allowed his charitable endeavours to wreak financial havoc on his own affairs. He clearly was an extremely generous man and, sadly, a great many people were aware, and duly took advantage of that undeniable fact.

With sound financial control, Elvis could, and should, have formed his own independent film company. This was a practice not unusual for stars in and before the 1960s. Other actors had formed companies which apart from the appeal of potentially higher financial rewards, gave them a controlling interest whereby they could have a much greater say in the selection of scripts, directors, technicians, co-stars and so on.

Some of the stars and their respective companies were: Steve McQueen, Solar Productions; James Garner, Cherokee Productions; Clint Eastwood, The Malpaso Company; and Cliff Robertson, Robertson Associates. To be involved in your own film company must be a great incentive for an actor, and I am convinced that had this opportunity been presented to

Elvis Presley, then his entire approach to film-making would have been radically changed.

Some of the actors just discussed have produced and/or directed their own films – doubtless a result of their feeling a new sense of authority over their own companies and a personal desire for expansion into acting's associated areas. Elvis's one foray into this particular aspect of cinematic progression began and ended in 1974, when it was announced that he was to star in and produce a documentary film on the subject of karate – a discipline for which Elvis had an undying passion. That year coincided with his obtaining an eighth-degree black belt in the art – a fact of which he was deservedly proud.

The karate project, to be titled *The New Gladiators* did commence filming. Elvis along with his close friend and karate mentor Ed Parker had undertaken a number of lectures and demonstrations of which a certain amount of footage was filmed. For some reason the project was shelved and remains incomplete. Had this reached fruition, it would have been a wonderful *coup* for Elvis to have himself, for the first time credited as producer of a film. It may have led to a greater desire for artistic fulfilment, and maybe one day Elvis might even have attempted what is generally considered the actor's ultimate goal – to direct his own films. Frank Sinatra had directed himself in *None but the Brave* (1965) and had served as producer on a number of his own films.

Joe Esposito, Elvis's long-time friend and business manager, made this interesting statement in his 'Elvis' Home Movies' video tape release:

> Elvis loved making movies at the beginning. But after the years they started getting to become the same movies. Different location, different girl, different kid, different animals. So that's why eventually he stopped making movies. He wanted to continue making movies later on but he wanted to direct movies. He always thought about in the future of being a director of action films. He loved action movies, or comedies. And that's one of the reasons he stopped making movies.

The year was also 1974 when Elvis made his last serious attempt to return to the cinema screen, with a drastically different image. Unlike the incomplete documentary, this karate story was a work of fiction. A dramatic story had been commissioned and was drafted by writer Rick Husky to display Elvis's proficiency in the martial arts. In the story Elvis was to play a retired CIA agent who becomes involved in a drugs case. On this occasion, unfortunately, no filming commenced. The project got no further than the written version. Even as late as 1974, it seems that Colonel Parker still regarded such intentions as potentially harmful to Elvis's image. This was of course ludicrous. The Elvis Presley of 1974 was far removed from that of the 1960s and it would have been essential to reflect this shift in any new screen characterization. Alas, it appeared that the Colonel won the point, and Elvis's iconoclastic rumblings were stilled.

In 1973, just one year prior to all this activity, it was mooted that Elvis should star in yet another martial arts film – this time uniting him with the legendary Bruce Lee, who alone was responsible for the commercial acceptability and subsequent success of films in that genre. In the book *Bruce Lee – King of Kung Fu* by Felix Dennis and Don Atyeo it was stated: 'During these troubled times, movie offers had continued to pour into the Golden Harvest offices. MGM wanted Lee to co-star opposite Elvis Presley (himself a martial arts disciple).' This would have been a most interesting vehicle for Elvis had it been made, and, considering the popularity of such films then, would almost definitely have been a major success. It is clear from the extract that Bruce Lee was not interested in appearing beside any established names, and his early death in July 1973 put paid once and for all to any such possibilities.

This was not the first occasion that someone had had the idea of teaming Elvis Presley with another prominent name. In the December 1969 issue of *Films and Filming*, Hal Wallis commented:

The Presley films were made, of course, for strictly commercial purposes. He is one of the most popular entertainers in the world and the films were most successful, but you have to give the Presley fans, who are legion, what they want, and they want to hear him sing. Probably, I wouldn't say the least successful because I don't have all the figures, but one of the least successful films was *King Creole* which was my favourite. Michael Curtiz directed it, and he has a very sharp and romantic instinct. Walter Matthau made an excellent heavy and we had marvellous locations in New Orleans. It was adapted from a book by Harold Robbins, but the songs were completely integral to the story. But we went on to make others – *Blue Hawaii* was probably the biggest grosser, and that's what the fans wanted. Working with Presley was a very pleasant experience: over the years I never had any problems with him. He did want to do some straight acting roles without any songs, but that would have been quite a gamble. He recently made one, *Charro!* – it'll be interesting to see how that goes.

Colonel Parker, his manager, is a good friend of mine, and he never bothered me about scripts. We gave him the starting date, I sent over the script and he said: 'If you want to do it, it's alright by me.' I never had any problems of rejecting stories or bringing up something else or anything of that kind, or 'We want to do a picture without songs', I never had that situation. Now, we could have gambled, probably and put him in a straight acting part, and even today, with the proper story and the proper set-up, I might do something of that kind. I had a story a while back that I was playing around with, for John Wayne and Presley; where Wayne was the old gunfighter and he picked up this boy and he was the young gunfigher, and if that could be developed it would be a good story and could be done without music.

Elvis Presley and John Wayne (the King and the Duke, no less) could have formed a truly formidable screen partnership. It is sad that for whatever reason, it was not to be. Elvis had also been offered a role in the first 'Cinerama' production (a simultaneous, triple projection system) in 1962, the sprawling (and flawed) *How the West Was Won*, which had featured Wayne among a whole coterie of leading actors. It was this very quantity of talent that was responsible for Elvis's non-appearance in the film. Colonel Parker apparently felt that Elvis's name would have been overshadowed by so many film industry luminaries in one production.

From his entrance into Hollywood filmdom until the last years of his life, Elvis Presley was sought to star with notable players in a variety of films – some of the vehicles prominent, others less so.

The Academy Award-winning Stanley Kramer film, *The Defiant Ones* (1958), which starred Tony Curtis and Sidney Poitier, should have starred Elvis Presley and Sammy Davis jun., according to the latter in his book *Hollywood in a Suitcase*. The diminutive star is a self-confessed cinema devotee, and in his book he describes engagingly the great many people and places with which he has come into contact in his long career as a singer, dancer and actor. Recounting the story of what went wrong regarding the Kramer film, he said:

> A great disappointment in my life came when it was seriously suggested that Elvis Presley and I should play the leads in *The Defiant Ones*. Both Elvis and I were keen to do the picture, but Elvis's manager Colonel Tom Parker thought it was 'controversial' as a vehicle for 'his boy' and turned it down. We both put up a terrific fight, but by the time everything got settled, we had gone on to other things. It was a shame because both of us would have been wonderful in the parts, and we would all have recognised at last, Elvis's burning ambition and ability to act his butt off.

Of Elvis's vast knowledge of films, Sammy Davis jun. said: 'It would be dificult to name the most ardent movie buff in the world. Buddy Rich and Elvis Presley could always give me a run for my money.'

Speaking of Elvis's artistic frustration, he added:

> Presley himself was always an enigma. He had a great talent as a screen personality and a couple of the things he did, like *King Creole* and *Kid Galahad* showed genuine promise. But they put him in that million-dollars-a-picture mould for the teenyboppers, and Colonel Tom wouldn't let him change. I know that Presley got fed up with it. After twenty or so

A lavish production – the prototype for many future musicals. This film earned more than any other Elvis Presley picture.
BLUE HAWAII

pictures he refused to make another one. 'I've done it all already. I can't go on making the same film over and over again,' he told me.

Presley had serious but gradual ambitions to become a 'real' actor. He became extremely frustrated when no-one would let him. A year or so before he died, we regularly sat all night together in Vegas and he'd pour his heart out about how he wanted to do a film without a single song. He was a great movie buff and we'd sit from midnight to dawn showing old movies. His own library was equal to my own and he had a wonderful ability for impersonation. His Bogey was better than mine ...

Presley was philosophical about his artistic frustration. 'How can I moan when I'm still making ten million dollars a year?' he said in Vegas, 'I'm still packing places. I've got no right to bitch.' He couldn't fight it and go out and do two shows a night.

I don't rate the spate of books that came out after Presley's death. They showed him as a morose man, bedevilled with fears and doubts. That was certainly not the Presley I knew. He had a great sense of humour and he was always full of fun. I guess all stars have their down periods, even deep depressions, and I don't think he was any different. But when I was around Elvis, they were all good times. We had a ball. There were no brooding depressions. He was the original plain guy made good. He really was a good, open-hearted country boy. His only frustration was that he needed to stretch himself more. After his entourage and the public between them had forced an image upon him, he had to lock himself into a private frame to be himself. Unlike me, he was never allowed the flexibility he needed as an artist.

All this was sterling praise indeed from one talented professional to another. Coincidentally, Sammy Davis jun.'s comments were reiterated by British actor Alan Bates in a 1978 interview for the Glasgow *Evening Times* when he said: 'I aim for total freedom of expression. Nureyev has it. Presley had it. Elvis was almost submerged by junk, taken over by his entourage and his image. But despite it all he was a great natural performer who gave freely of himself.'

Numerous projects were mentioned over the years that Elvis Presley, for one reason or another, did not appear in. It was rumoured in 1965 that he would play Hank Williams in MGM's *Your Cheating Heart*, but George Hamilton took the part. In 1967 he was to make a suspense thriller entitled *Follow That Bird*, to be produced by Hal Landers and Bobby Roberts, the team who later produced *Death Wish* (1974). Nothing more was heard of it. A spy film called *That Jack Valentine* or *The Jack Valentine Story* was announced in 1968, but never appeared. A western project, *A Hard Ride*, was rumoured for 1969. The news sank without trace. Several reports stated that Elvis had turned down the role of Joe Buck (for which Jon Voight received an Academy Award nomination) in John Schlesinger's *Midnight Cowboy*.

Photoplay film magazine stated in their November 1971 issue that Elvis was to make a film with Mia Farrow called *Damnation Walk* for 20th Century Fox. This received no further mention. Yet another western was slated for 1972, *Remnants of the Old West* and, once again, no more was heard of it.

Grease (eventually a huge hit in 1978) was mentioned in a US movie magazine as a possible vehicle for Elvis at Paramount studios in 1973. Wouldn't Elvis, at age thirty-eight have seemed a touch out of place in a high-school story? One of the strangest vehicles proposed was something called *Man on the Moon*, reported in 1974. Film director Paul Morrissey apparently had talks with Elvis in Hollywood regarding this project, which had been written by John Phillips of The Mamas and Papas fame. The storyline was said to be 'a musical fantasy about a little girl who goes to the moon and meets an American astronaut'. Curiouser and curiouser.

Announcements in 1975 included a proposed musical version by producer Ray Stark of his 1960 film *The World of Suzie Wong*. This did not materialize, of course, but a statement in the *Monthly Film Bulletin* upon the original film's release was indeed prophetic: It said, 'Maybe one day it will make the grade as a musical.' That same year, Elvis was reported to be about to embark on a project called *The Gospel Singer*, with himself as the producer and his great friend

Tom Jones as the star. In another later report concerning this film, it was stated that producer Larry Spangler had offered Elvis $1 million plus fifty per cent of the profits to star in *The Gospel Singer*. Whatever the machinations, the film was never made.

Late-1975 brought news of a promoter attempting to acquire Elvis's services for a stage performance as Valentino at the Radio City Music Hall in New York. An off-shoot idea was to film one of the performances, which were hoped to run for a six-week engagement, and release the resulting movie to cinemas worldwide. A very strange idea, and yet another film which did not get off the ground.

In 1975 Elvis was also offered the male lead in what proved to be a mega-hit movie, *A Star is Born* with Barbra Streisand. Turning down the film was probably the greatest cinematic mistake Elvis ever made. The finished film was a superbly made example of a modern musical drama. The quest for Elvis Presley as co-star was first made public in March 1975 when Barbra Streisand stated in an interview that she wanted Elvis for the film. She said: 'He would be super. He's a very talented actor. I would be an aspiring actress and Elvis would be my mentor. I just don't know if Elvis would mind being eclipsed though.' That same month, at the royal film performance of her then latest film *Funny Lady*, Ms Streisand stated: 'We're hoping to get Elvis Presley for the film, but we haven't actually asked him yet. The papers misquoted me and said that Elvis Presley was to be the star, but we had not approached him even. I hope he is not offended. The script is not yet finished, and when it's complete, we will send it to him.'

Streisand later met with Elvis at the Las Vegas Hilton Hotel and unfolded the plans for her project. Elvis, it seemed, was enthusiastic, but because of Colonel Parker's intervention and discontent over the financial arrangements, Elvis did not commit himself. Eventually, after waiting for some time, Streisand contracted Kris Kristofferson to play the part. The influence that Colonel Parker seemed to have over Elvis was incredible. His close friends claimed that Elvis was a decisive, temperamental, strong-willed man, and yet he frequently succumbed to Parker's requests. Perhaps it was respect, perhaps it was undying gratitude, but it caused Elvis Presley immeasurable damage to his career. An excellent screen opportunity was lost to him because of the dissatisfaction of his manager.

Kris Kristofferson (whose own music Elvis admired and had recorded) was impressive as the has-been rock idol in *A Star is Born*, but Elvis could have been terrific in the role, and it could well have satisfied his avowed creative desires. Kristofferson went on to a degree of success as a leading film actor, and the irony of the comparison is that he appeared in his first film role in Dennis Hopper's *The Last Movie* (1971), when he was thirty-five years old. Elvis, at the same age, had all but ended his long reign as a major film star – with almost three dozen movies completed (one documentary was still to come, when he was thirty-seven).

Following the great disappointment for his admirers of Elvis's refusal to accept the role in the Streisand film, no further rumours, announcements or projects were ever mentioned for him as a cinema actor.

Comments regarding Elvis Presley from others in the world of film were conflicting. Tony Curtis stated more than once that he was considered the worst actor in Hollywood until Elvis Presley came along. By contrast, producer Mike Frankovich said in 1969: 'If I were doing a remake of *Gone with the Wind*, I'd cast Elvis in the Rhett Butler role – and it wouldn't be a musical, either. Elvis Presley is the only young actor around with that rare Clark Gable quality.'

Colonel Parker's involvement with Elvis Presley's film career, other than being instrumental in arranging contracts, caused him to be listed as 'Technical Advisor' on the credits of almost every Presley film – a most curious title to be bestowed upon him. Such a description suggested that he was knowledgeable about film-making techniques, and in that capacity, gave advice to those in need. I am quite convinced that Colonel Parker had no inkling of technical know-how, and that possibly he contractually demanded the inclusion of this egotistical title.

One of the clear and continuing problems with Elvis's films

was the frequent participation, on the production side (writers, producers, directors), of motion picture veterans – men too old and out of step with modern approaches. On the one hand, their experience was a considerable asset to a production in terms of professionalism, but on the other hand this same input kept Elvis Presley in a limiting screen area. His films became out of touch with their period. Elvis had no clear direction in which to go. Although there have been in the past, and still are today, masterful film directors and producers of an advanced age, the last twenty years or so have seen the emergence of a younger breed – men who are cognizant of the needs of today's cinema-goers. Had Elvis's projects been graced with the talents of younger, innovative film-makers, then the end result could have been vastly different.

British journalist Ray Connolly was granted an interview with Elvis in Las Vegas at the time of the triumphant 1969 stage return, and of his Hollywood days Elvis commented:

> We've now completed all the deals I made when I came out of the army in 1960, and from now on I'm going to play more serious parts and make fewer films. I wouldn't be being honest with you if I said I wasn't ashamed of some of the movies and the songs I've had to sing in them. I would like to say they were good, but I can't. I've been extremely unhappy with that side of my career for some time. But how can you find twelve good songs for every film when you're making three films a year? I knew a lot of them were bad songs and they used to bother the heck out of me. But I had to do them. They fitted the situation.

Elvis's disenchantment with his films was more than obvious by now, and he was honest enough to admit to their inferiority. Hal Wallis's comments about never having problems with scripts or anything else was clearly indicative of Elvis's inexplicable acceptance of this below-average material. His acting talent remained largely untapped, through a measure of his own failure to demand changes and a combination of greed and gross ineptitude by his so-called advisors.

Throughout his long film career, after it had ended and even following his death, Elvis was the victim of inimical critical attack. To critics and a large section of the public he was considered a non-actor. If Elvis was a nondescript screen performer and not the quintessential Hollywood actor, then just who was? What is the correct criterion? Commercially, Elvis Presley had far greater success than several Academy Award winning actors. Which, of those two categories, can be considered the greater failure?

The fact is that Elvis Presley, not totally at ease in a secondary industry (music was, after all, his greatest talent and his first love), left decisions to others whom he thought knew best. What resulted was that he was sold out artistically by those in whose trust he placed himself. Where and when possible, he gave openly of his talent. Hollywood, to a large extent, failed to reciprocate. True, Elvis Presley earned millions of dollars from Hollywood, but Hollywood earned millions more from him. The lesson here is never to commit yourself fully to an unknown industry, and relinquish personal control. Elvis Presley learned that lesson too late.

I was the hero of the comic book, I saw movies and I was the hero of the movie. So every dream that I ever dreamed has come true a hundred times.

Part of Elvis Presley's acceptance speech
upon receiving the US Jaycees Award as one
of the 'Ten Most Outstanding Young Men of America'
in Memphis, January 1971.

A Complete Filmography

Love Me Tender (1956)

Studio: 20th Century Fox
Director: Robert D. Webb
Producer: David Weisbart
Screenplay: Robert Buckner
Story: Maurice Geraghty
Photography: Leo Tover ASC

Editor Hugh S. Fowler
Music: Lionel Newman
Vocal supervision: Ken Darby
Art Direction: Lyle R. Wheeler and Maurice Ransford
Costumes: Mary Wills

Cast: Vance (Richard Egan), Cathy (Debra Paget), Clint (Elvis Presley), Siringo (Robert Middleton), Brett Reno (William Campbell), Mike Gavin (Neville Brand), the mother (Mildred Dunnock) Major Kincaid (Bruce Bennett), Ray Reno (James Drury), Ed Galt (Russ Conway), Kelso (Ken Clark), Davis (Barry Coe), Fleming (L.Q. Jones), Jethro (Paul Burns), train conductor (Jerry Sheldon).

(*Running time*: 89 mins)

Loving You (1957)

Elvis looks on with interest as a scene is deliberated. This role was a brief return to his aggressive persona; Barbara Stanwyck proved a formidable co-star. ROUSTABOUT

Studio: Paramount
Director: Hal Kanter
Producer: Hal B. Wallis
Screenplay: Herbert Baker and Hal Kanter
Story: Mary Agnes Thompson
Photography: Charles Lang jun. ASC

Editor: Howard Smith ACE
Music: Walter Scharf
Vocal accompaniment: The Jordanaires
Art Direction: Hal Pereira and Albert Nozaki
Costumes: Edith Head

Cast: Deke Rivers (Elvis Presley), Glenda Markle (Lizabeth Scott), Walter 'Tex' Warner (Wendell Corey), Susan Jessup (Dolores Hart), Carl (James Gleason), Tallman (Ralph Dumke), Skeeter (Paul Smith), Wayne, (Ken Becker) Daisy (Jana Lund). *(Running time*: 101 mins)

Jailhouse Rock (1957)

Studio: Metro-Goldwyn-Mayer
Director: Richard Thorpe
Producer: Pandro S. Berman
Screenplay: Guy Trosper
Story: Ned Young

Photography: Robert Bronner ASC
Editor: Ralph E. Winters
Music: Jeff Alexander
Art direction: William A. Horning and Randell Duell

Cast: Vince Everett (Elvis Presley), Peggy Van Alden (Judy Tyler), Hunk Houghton (Mickey Shaughnessy), Mr Shores (Vaughan Taylor), Sherry Wilson (Jennifer Holden), Teddy Talbot (Dean Jones), Laury Jackson (Ann Neyland), Warden (Hugh Sanders). *(Running time*: 96 mins)

King Creole (1958)

Studio: Paramount
Director: Michael Curtiz
Producer: Hal B. Wallis
Screenplay: Herbert Baker and Michael Vincente Gazzo
Story: based on the novel *A Stone for Danny Fisher* by Harold Robbins.

Photography: Russell Harlan ASC
Editor: Warren Low ACE
Music: Walter Scharf
Vocal accompaniment: The Jordanaires
Art direction: Hal Pereira and Joseph MacMillan Johnson
Costumes: Edith Head

Cast: Danny Fisher (Elvis Presley), Ronnie (Carolyn Jones), Nellie (Dolores Hart), Mr Fisher (Dean Jagger), 'Forty' Nina (Liliane Montevecchi), Maxie Fields (Walter Matthau), Mimi (Jan Shepard), Charlie LeGrand (Paul Stewart), Shark (Vic Morrow), Sal (Brian Hutton).

(Running time: 115 mins)

GI Blues (1960)

Studio: Paramount
Director: Norman Taurog
Producer: Hal B. Wallis
Associate producer: Paul Nathan
Screenplay: Edmund Beloin and Henry Garson
Photography: Loyal Griggs ASC
Editor: Warren Low ACE

Music: Joseph J. Lilley
Vocal accompaniment: The Jordanaires
Art direction: Hal Pereira and Walter Tyler
Costumes: Edith Head
Military Advisor: Captain David S. Parkhurst

Cast: Tulsa MacLean (Elvis Presley), Lili (Juliet Prowse), Cooky (Robert Ivers), Tina (Leticia Roman), Rick (James Douglas), Marla (Sigrid Maier), Sergeant McGraw (Arch Johnson). (*Running time*: 104 mins)

Flaming Star (1960)

Studio: 20th Century Fox
Director: Don Siegel
Producer: David Weisbart
Screenplay: Clair Huffaker and Nunnally Johnson
Story: Clair Huffaker
Photography: Charles G. Clarke ASC

Editor: Hugh S. Fowler
Music: Cyril J. Mockridge/ conducted by Lionel Newman
Vocal accompaniment: The Jordanaires
Choreography: Josephine Earl
Art direction: Duncan Cramer and Walter M. Simonds
Costumes: Adele Balkan

Cast: Pacer Burton (Elvis Presley), Roslyn Pierce (Barbara Eden), Clint Burton (Steve Forrest), Neddy Burton (Dolores del Rio), Pa Burton (John McIntire), Buffalo Horn (Rudolph Acosta), Dred Pierce (Karl Swenson), Doc Phillips (Ford Rainey), Angus Pierce (Richard Jaeckel), Dorothy Howard (Anne Benton), Tom Howard (L.Q. Jones), Will Howard (Douglas Dick), Jute (Tom Reese), Ph'Sha Knay (Marian Goldina), Ben Ford (Monte Burkhart), Hornsby (Ted Jacques), Indian brave (Rodd Redwing), Two Moons (Perry Lopez) (*Running time*: 101 mins)

Wild in the Country (1960)

Studio: 20th Century Fox
Director: Philip Dunne
Producer: Jerry Wald
Associate producer: Peter Nelson
Screenplay: Clifford Odets
Story: based on the novel *The Lost Country* by J.R. Salamanca
Photography: William C. Mellor ASC
Editor: Dorothy Spencer
Music: Kenyon Hopkins
Art direction: Jack Martin Smith and Preston Ames
Costumes: Don Feld

Cast: Glenn Tyler (Elvis Presley), Irene Sperry (Hope Lange) Noreen (Tuesday Weld), Betty Lee (Millie Perkins), Davis (Rafer Johnson), Phil Macy (John Ireland), Cliff Macy (Gary Lockwood), Uncle Rolfe (William Mims), Dr Underwood (Raymond Greenleaf), Monica George (Christina Crawford), Flossie (Robin Raymond), Mrs Parsons (Doreen Lang), Mr Parsons (Charles Arnt), Sarah (Ruby Goodwin), Willie Dace (Will Corry), Professor Larson (Alan Napier), Judge Parker (Jason Robards, sen.), bartender (Harry Carter), Sam Tyler (Harry Shannon), Hank Tyler (Bobby West).

(Running time: 114 mins)

Blue Hawaii (1961)

Studio: Paramount
Director: Norman Taurog
Producer: Hal B. Wallis
Associate producer: Paul Nathan
Screenplay: Hal Kanter
Story: Allan Weiss
Photography: Charles Lang jun. ASC
Editors: Warren Low and Terry Morse ACE
Music: Joseph J. Lilley
Vocal accompaniment: The Jordanaires
Choreography: Charles O'Curran
Art direction: Hal Pereira and Walter Tyler
Costumes: Edith Head

Cast: Chad Gates (Elvis Presley), Maile Duval (Joan Blackman), Abigail Prentace (Nancy Walters), Sarah Lee Gates (Angela Lansbury) Fred Gates (Roland Winters), Jack Kelman (John Archer), Mr Chapman (Howard McNear), Mrs Manaka (Flora Hayes), Mr Duval (Gregory Gay), Mr Garvey (Steve Brodie), Mrs Garvey (Iris Adrian), Patsy (Darlene Tompkins), Sandy (Pamela Kirk), Beverly (Christina Kay), Ellie (Jenny Maxwell), Ito O'Hara (Frank Atienza), Carl (Lani Kai), Ernie (Jose De Varga), Wes (Ralph Hanalie).

(Running time: 101 mins)

Follow That Dream (1961)

Studio: United Artists
Director: Gordon Douglas
Producer: David Weisbart
Screenplay: Charles Lederer
Story: based on the novel *Pioneer,* *Go Home* by Richard Powell
Photography: Leo Tover ASC
Editor: William B. Murphy ACE
Music: Hans J. Salter
Art direction: Malcolm Bert

Cast: Toby Kwimper (Elvis Presley), Pop Kwimper (Arthur O'Connell), Holly Jones (Anne Helm), Alicia Claypoole (Joanna Moore), Carmine (Jack Kruschen), Nick (Simon Oakland), Eddy and Teddy Bascombe (Gavin and Robin Koon), the governor (Harry Holcombe), Ariadne Pennington (Pam Ogles), the judge (Roland Winters), Endicott (Herbert Rudley), H. Arthur King (Alan Hewitt), George (Howard McNear), Jack (Frank De Cova), Blackie (John Duke), Al (Robert Carricart).

(*Running time*: 110 mins)

Kid Galahad (1961)

Studio: United Artists
Director: Phil Karlson
Producer: David Weisbart
Screenplay: William Fay
Story: based on the novel *Kid Galahad* by Francis Wallace
Photography: Burnett Guffey ASC
Editor: Stuart Gilmore
Music: Jeff Alexander
Art direction: Cary Odell
Costumes: Bert Henrickson and Irene Caine
Boxing advisor: Mushy Callahan

Cast: Walter Gulick (Elvis Presley), Willy Grogan (Gig Young) Dolly Fletcher (Lola Albright), Rose Grogan (Joan Blackman), Lew Nyack (Charles Bronson), Lieberman (Ned Glass), Maynard (Robert Emhardt), Otto Danzig (David Lewis), Joie Shakes (Michael Dante), Zimmerman (Judson Pratt), Sperling (George Mitchell), Marvin (Richard Devon), Ralphie (Jeffrey Morris), Father Higgins (Liam Redmond), Pete Prohosko (Ralph Moody), Ramon 'Sugar Boy' Romero (Ramon de la Fuente).

(*Running time*: 97 mins)

Girls! Girls! Girls! (1962)

Studio: Paramount
Director: Norman Taurog
Producer: Hal B. Wallis
Associate producer: Paul Nathan
Screenplay: Edward Anhalt and Allan Weiss
Story: Allan Weiss

Photography: Loyal Griggs ASC
Editor: Warren Low ACE
Music: Joseph J. Lilley
Choreography: Charles O'Curran
Art direction: Hal Pereira and Walter Tyler
Costumes: Edith Head

Cast: Ross Carpenter (Elvis Presley), Robin Gantner (Stella Stevens), Laurel Dodge (Laurel Goodwin), Wesley Johnson (Jeremy Slate), Chen Yung (Guy Lee), Kin Yung (Benson Fong), Madame Yung (Beulah Quo), Alexander Stavros (Frank Puglia), Mama Stavros (Lili Valenty), Sam (Robert Strauss), Leona and Linda Stavros (Barbara and Betty Beall), Mai and Tai Ling (Ginny and Elizabeth Tiu), Arthur Morgan (Nestor Paiva), Mrs Morgan (Ann McCrea).

(*Running time*: 106 mins)

It Happened at the World's Fair (1962)

Studio: Metro-Goldwyn-Mayer
Director: Norman Taurog
Producer: Ted Richmond
Screenplay: Si Rose and Seaman Jacobs
Photography: Joseph Ruttenberg ASC
Editor: Frederic Steinkamp

Music: Leith Stevens
Vocal accompaniment: The Jordanaires and the Mello Men
Choreography: Jack Baker
Art direction: George W. Davis and Preston Ames
Costumes: Elvis Presley's clothes designed by Sy Devore

Cast: Mike Edwards (Elvis Presley), Diane Warren (Joan O'Brien), Danny Burke (Gary Lockwood), Sue-Lin (Vicky Tiu), Vince Bradley (H.M. Wynant), Miss Steuben (Edith Atwater), Barney Thatcher (Guy Raymond), Miss Ettinger (Dorothy Green), Walter Ling (Kam Tong), Dorothy Johnson (Yvonne Craig), Mr Johnson (Olan Soule), Mrs Johnson (Jacqueline De Witt), boy at fair (Kurt Russell).

(*Running time*: 105 mins)

Fun in Acapulco (1963)

Studio: Paramount
Director: Richard Thorpe
Producer: Hal B. Wallis
Associate producer: Paul Nathan
Screenplay: Allan Weiss
Photography: Daniel L. Fapp ASC
Editor: Warren Low ACE

Music: Joseph J. Lilley
Vocal accompaniment: the Jordanaires and the Four Amigos
Choreography: Charles O'Curran
Art direction: Hal Pereira and Walter Tyler
Costumes: Edith Head

Cast: Mike Windgren (Elvis Presley), Margarita Dauphine (Ursula Andress), Dolores Gomez (Elsa Cardenas), Maximilian (Paul Lukas), Raoul Almeido (Larry Domasin), Moreno (Alejandro Rey), Jose (Robert Carricart), Janie Harkins (Teri Hope), Mr Harkins (Charles Evans), hotel manager (Alberto Morin), desk clerk (Francisco Ortega), bellboy (Robert De Anda), telegraph clerk (Linda Rivera), first girl (Darlene Tompkins), second girl (Linda Rand), musicians (Eddie Cano, Carlos Mejia, Leon Cardenas, Fred Aguirre), photographer (Tom Hernandez), secretary (Adele Palacios). *(Running time*: 98 mins)

Viva Las Vegas (1963)
(UK title: Love in Las Vegas)

Studio: Metro-Goldwyn-Mayer
Director: George Sidney
Producers: Jack Cummings and George Sidney
Screenplay: Sally Benson
Photography: Joseph Biroc ASC

Editor: John McSweeney ACE
Music: George Stoll
Choreography: David Winters
Art direction: George W. Davis and Edward Carfagno
Costumes: Don Feld

Cast: Lucky Jackson (Elvis Presley), Rusty Martin (Ann-Margret), Count Elmo Mancini (Cesare Danova), Mr Martin (William Demarest), Shorty Farnsworth (Nicky Blair). *(Running Time*: 86 mins)

Kissin' Cousins (1963)

Studio: Metro-Goldwyn-Mayer
Director: Gene Nelson
Producer: Sam Katzman
Screenplay: Gerald Drayson Adams and Gene Nelson
Story: Gerald Drayson Adams

Photography: Ellis W. Carter ASC
Editor: Ben Lewis
Music: Fred Karger
Choreography: Hal Belfer
Art direction: George W. Davis and Eddie Imazu

Cast: Josh Morgan/Jodie Tatum (Elvis Presley), Pappy Tatum (Arthur O'Connell), Ma Tatum (Glenda Farrell), Captain Robert Salbo (Jack Albertson), Selina Tatum (Pam Austin), Midge (Cynthia Pepper), Azalea Tatum (Yvonne Craig), General Alvin Donford (Donald Woods), Master-Sergeant Bailey (Tommy Farrell), Trudy (Beverly Powers), Dixie (Hortense Petra), General's aide (Robert Stone).

(Running time: 96 mins)

Roustabout (1964)

Studio: Paramount
Director: John Rich
Producer: Hal B. Wallis
Associate producer: Paul Nathan
Screenplay: Anthony Lawrence and Allan Weiss
Story: Allan Weiss

Photography: Lucien Ballard ASC
Editor: Warren Low ACE
Music: Joseph J. Lilley
Choreography: Earl Barton
Art direction: Hal Pereira and Walter Tyler
Costumes: Edith Head

Cast: Charlie Rogers (Elvis Presley), Maggie Morgan (Barbara Stanwyck), Cathy Lean (Joan Freeman), Joe Lean (Leif Erickson), Madame Mijanou (Sue Ane Langdon), Harry Carver (Pat Buttram), Marge (Joan Staley), Arthur Nielsen (Dabs Greer), Fred (Steve Brodie), College Student (Norman Grabowski), Lou (Jack Albertson), Hazel (Jane Dulo), Cody Marsh (Joel Fluellen), Little Egypt (Wilda Taylor), Midget (Billy Barty), college student (Raquel Welch).

(Running time: 101 mins)

Girl Happy (1964)

Studio: Metro-Goldwyn-Mayer
Director: Boris Sagal
Producer: Joe Pasternak
Screenplay: Harvey Bullock and R.S. Allen
Photography: Philip Lathrop ASC
Editor: Rita Roland
Music: George Stoll
Vocal accompaniment: The Jordanaires
Choreography: David Winters
Art direction: George W. Davis and Addison Hehr
Costumes: Don Feld

Cast: Rusty Wells (Elvis Presley), Valerie (Shelley Fabares), Big Frank (Harold J. Stone), Andy (Gary Crosby), Wilbur (Joby Baker), Sunny Daze (Nita Talbot), Deena (Mary Ann Mobley), Romano (Fabrizio Mioni), Doc (Jimmy Hawkins), Sergeant Benson (Jackie Coogan), Brentwood Von Durgenfield (Peter Brooks), Mr Penchill (John Fiedler), Betsy (Chris Noel), Laurie (Lyn Edgington), Nancy (Gail Gilmore), Bobbie (Pamela Curran), Linda (Rusty Allen), 'wolf-call' student (Norman Grabowski), police captain (Milton Frome), police officer (Richard Reeves).

(*Running time*: 96 mins)

Tickle Me (1964)

Studio: Allied Artists Picture Corporation
Director: Norman Taurog
Producer: Ben Schwalb
Screenplay: Elwood Ullman and Edward Bernds
Photography: Loyal Griggs ASC
Editor: Archie Marshek ACE
Music: Walter Scharf
Vocal accompaniment: The Jordanaires
Choreography: David Winters
Art Direction: Hal Pereira and Arthur Lonergan
Costumes: Leah Rhodes

Cast: Lonnie Beale (Elvis Presley), Vera Radford (Julie Adams), Pam Merritt (Jocelyn Lane), Stanley Potter (Jack Mullaney), Estelle Penfield (Merry Anders), Deputy Sturdivant (Bill Williams), Brad Bentley (Edward Faulkner), Hilda (Connie Gilchrist) Barbara (Barbara Werle), Adolph (John Dennis), Mr Dabney (Grady Sutton), Mabel (Allison Hayes), Ophelia (Inez Pedroza), Ronnie (Lilyan Chauvin), Donna (Angela Greene).

(*Running time*: 90 mins)

Harum Scarum (1965)
(UK title: Harem Holiday)

Studio: Metro-Goldwyn-Mayer
Director: Gene Nelson
Producer: Sam Katzman
Screenplay: Gerald Drayson Adams
Photography: Fred H. Jackman
Editor: Ben Lewis

Music: Fred Karger
Vocal accompaniment: The Jordanaires
Choreography: Earl Barton
Art direction: George W. Davis and H. McClure Capps

Cast: Johnny Tyronne (Elvis Presley), Princess Shalimar (Mary Ann Mobley), Aishah (Fran Jeffries), Prince Dragna (Michael Ansara), Zacha (Jay Novello), King Toranshah (Philip Reed), Sinan (Theo Marcuse), Baba (Billy Barty), Mokar (Dick Harvey), Julna (Jack Costanzo), Captain Herat (Larry Chance), Leilah (Barbara Werle), Emerald (Brenda Benet), Sapphire (Gail Gilmore), Amethyst (Wilda Taylor), Sari (Vicki Malkin), Mustapha (Rick Rydon), scarred bedouin (Richard Reeves), Yussef (Jerry Rousso).

(Running Time: 85 mins)

Frankie and Johnny (1965)

Studio: United Artists
Director: Frederick de Cordova
Producer: Edward Small
Associate producer/Screenplay: Alex Gottlieb
Story: Nat Perrin

Photography: Jacques Marquette ASC
Editor Grant Whytock
Music: Fred Karger
Choreography: Earl Barton
Art direction: Walter Simonds

Costumes: Gwen Wakeling

Cast: Johnny (Elvis Presley), Frankie (Donna Douglas), Cully (Harry Morgan), Peg (Audrey Christie), Nellie Bly (Nancy Kovack), Mitzi (Sue Ane Langdon), Blackie (Robert Strauss), Braden (Anthony Eisley), Wilbur (Jerome Cowen), Earl Barton Dancers (Wilda Taylor, Larri Thomas, Dee Jay Mattis, Judy Chapman).

(Running time 87 mins)

Paradise, Hawaiian Style (1965)

Studio: Paramount
Director: Michael Moore
Producer: Hal B. Wallis
Assoiate producer: Paul Nathan
Screenplay: Allan Weiss and Anthony Lawrence
Story: Allan Weiss
Photography: W. Wallace Kelley ASC

Editor: Warren Low ACE
Music: Joseph J. Lilley
Vocal accompaniment: The Jordanaires
Choreography: Jack Regas
Art direction: Hal Pereira and Walter Tyler
Costumes: Edith Head

Cast: Rick Richards (Elvis Presley), Judy Hudson (Suzanna Leigh), Danny Kohana (James Shigeta), Jan Kohana (Donna Butterworth), Lani (Marianna Hill), Pua (Irene Tsu), Lehua (Linda Wong), Joanna (Julie Parrish), Betty Kohana (Jan Shepard), Donald Belden (John Doucette), Moki (Philip Ahn), Mr Cubberson (Grady Sutton), Andy Lowell (Don Collier), Mrs Barrington (Doris Packer), Mrs Belden (Mary Treen), Peggy Holden (Gigi Verone).

(Running time: 91 mins)

Spinout (1966)
(UK title: California Holiday)

Studio: Metro-Goldwyn-Mayer
Director: Norman Taurog
Producer: Joe Pasternak
Associate producer: Hank Moonjean
Screenplay: Theodore J. Flicker and George Kirgo

Editor: Rita Roland
Music: George Stoll
Vocal accompaniment: The Jordanaires
Choreography: Jack Baker
Art direction: George W. Davis and Edward Carfagno

Photography: Daniel L. Fapp ASC

Cast: Mike McCoy (Elvis Presley), Cynthia Foxhugh (Shelley Fabares), Diana St.Clair (Diane McBain), Les (Deborah Walley), Susan (Dodie Marshall), Curly (Jack Mullaney), Lt. Tracy Richards (Will Hutchins), Philip Short (Warren Berlinger), Larry (Jimmy Hawkins), Howard Foxhugh (Carl Betz), Bernard Ranley (Cecil Kellaway), Violet Ranley (Una Merkel), Blodgett (Frederick Worlock), Harry (Dave Barry).

(Running time: 93 mins)

Double Trouble (1966)

Studio: Metro-Goldwyn-Mayer
Director: Norman Taurog
Producers: Judd Bernard and Irwin Winkler
Screenplay: Jo Heims
Story: Marc Brandel
Photography: Daniel L. Fapp ASC
Editor: John McSweeney ACE
Music: Jeff Alexander
Choreography: Alex Romero
Art direction: George W. Davis and Merrill Pye
Costumes: Don Feld

Cast: Guy Lambert (Elvis Presley), Jill Conway (Annette Day), Gerald Waverly (John Williams), Claire Dunham (Yvonne Romain), The Weire brothers (themselves), Archie Brown (Chips Rafferty), Arthur Babcock (Norman Rossington), Georgie (Monty Landis), Morley (Michael Murphy), Inspector De Grotte (Leon Askin), iceman (John Alderson), Captain Roach (Stanley Adams), Frenchman (Maurice Marsac), mate (Walter Burke), Gerda (Helene Winston), The G-men (themselves).

(*Running time*: 92 mins)

Easy Come, Easy Go (1966)

Studio: Paramount
Director: John Rich
Producer: Hal B. Wallis
Associate producer: Paul Nathan
Screenplay: Allan Weiss and Anthony Lawrence
Photography: William Margulies ASC
Editor: Archie Marshek ACE
Music: Joseph J. Lilley
Vocal accompaniment: The Jordanaires
Choreography: David Winters
Art direction: Hal Pereira and Walter Tyler
Costumes: Edith Head

Cast: Ted Jackson (Elvis Presley), Jo Symington (Dodie Marshall), Dina Bishop (Pat Priest), Judd Whitman (Pat Harrington), Gil Corey (Skip Ward), Captain Jack (Frank McHugh), Cooper (Ed Griffith), Schwartz (Sandy Kenyon), Whitehead (Mickey Elley), Tompkins (Read Morgan), Vicki (Elaine Beckett), Mary (Shari Nims), Zoltan (Diki Lerner), artist (Robert Isenberg), Madame Neherina (Elsa Lanchester)

(*Running time*: 95 mins)

Clambake (1967)

Studio: United Artists
Director: Arthur Nadel
Producers: Arnold Laven, Arthur Gardner and Jules Levy
Associate producer: Tom Rolf
Screenplay: Arthur Browne jun.
Photography: William Margulies ASC
Editor: Tom Rolf
Music: Jeff Alexander
Choreography: Alex Romero
Art direction: Lloyd Papez

Cast: Scott Heyward (Elvis Presley), Dianne Carter (Shelley Fabares), Tom Wilson (Will Hutchins), James Jamison III (Bill Bixby), Duster Heyward (James Gregory), Ellie (Amanda Harley), Sally (Suzy Kaye), Gloria (Angelique Pettyjohn), Gigi (Olga Kaye), Olive (Arlene Charles), Mr Hathaway (Jack Good), doorman (Hal Peary), race announcer (Sam Riddle) cigarette girl (Sue England), Lisa (Lisa Slagle), bartender (Lee Krieger), crewman (Melvin Allen), waiter (Herb Barnett), bell hop (Steve Cory), Barasch (Robert Lieb), ice-cream vendor (Red West).

(*Running time*: 99 mins)

Speedway (1967)

Studio: Metro-Goldwyn-Mayer
Director: Norman Taurog
Producer: Douglas Laurence
Screenplay: Phillip Shuken
Photography: Joseph Ruttenberg ASC
Editor: Richard Farrell
Music: Jeff Alexander
Vocal accompaniment: The Jordanaires
Art direction: George W. Davis and Leroy Coleman

Cast: Steve Grayson (Elvis Presley), Susan Jacks (Nancy Sinatra), Kenny Donford (Bill Bixby), R.W. Hepworth (Gale Gordon), Abel Esterlake (William Schallert), Ellie Esterlake (Victoria Meyerink), Paul Dado (Ross Hagen), Birdie Kebner (Carl Ballantine), Juan Medala (Poncie Ponce), the cook (Harry Hickox), Billy Jo (Christopher West), Mary Ann (Miss Beverly Hills), Ted Simmons (Harper Carter), Lloyd Meadows (Bob Harris), Debbie (Michele Newman), Carrie (Courtney Brown), Billie (Dana Brown), Annie (Patti Jean Keith), Mike (Carl Reindel), dumb blonde (Gari Hardy), Lori (Charlotte Considine), race announcer (Sandy Reed).

(*Running time*: 94 mins)

Stay Away, Joe (1967)

Studio: Metro-Goldwyn-Mayer
Director: Peter Tewksbury
Producer: Douglas Laurence
Screenplay: Michael A. Hoey and Burt Kennedy (uncredited)
Story: based on the novel *Stay Away, Joe* by Dan Cushman

Photography: Fred Koenekamp ASC
Editor: George W. Brooks
Music: Jack Marshall
Vocal accompaniment: The Jordanaires
Art direction: George W. Davis and Carl Anderson

Cast: Joe Lightcloud (Elvis Presley), Charlie Lightcloud (Burgess Meredith), Glenda Callahan (Joan Blondell), Annie Lightcloud (Katy Jurado), Grandpa (Thomas Gomez), Hy Slager (Henry Jones), Bronc Hoverty (L.Q. Jones), Mamie Callahan (Quentin Dean), Mrs Hawkins (Anne Seymour), Congressman Morrissey (Douglas Henderson), Lorne Hawkins (Angus Duncan), Frank Hawk (Michael Lane), Mary Lightcloud (Susan Trustman), Hike Bowers (Warren Vanders), Bull Shortgun (Buck Kartalian), Connie Shortgun (Mourishka), Marlene Standing Rattle (Caitlin Wyles), Billie Jo Hump (Marya Christen), Jackson He-Crow (Del 'Sonny' West), Little Deer (Jennifer Peak), Deputy Sheriff Hank Matson (Brett Parker), Orville Witt (Michael Keller), salesman (Dick Wilson), Judge Nibley (Harry Harvey sen.) announcer (Robert Lieb).

(*Running time*: 100 mins)

Live a Little, Love a Little (1968)

Studio: Metro-Goldwyn-Mayer
Director: Norman Taurog
Producer: Douglas Laurence
Screenplay: Michael A. Hoey and Dan Greenburg
Story: based on the novel *Kiss my Firm but Pliant Lips* by Dan Greenburg

Photography: Fred Koenekamp ASC
Editor: John McSweeney ACE
Music: Billy Strange
Choreography: Jack Regas and Jack Baker
Art direction: George W. Davis and Preston Ames

Cast: Greg Nolan (Elvis Presley), Bernice (Michelle Carey), Mike Lansdown (Don Porter), Penlow (Rudy Vallee), Harry (Dick Sargent), milkman (Sterling Holloway),Ellen (Celeste Yarnall), delivery boy (Eddie Hodges), Robbie's mother (Joan Shawlee), Miss Selfridge (Mary Grover), receptionist (Emily Banks), art director (Michael Keller), first secretary (Merri Ashley), second secretary (Phyllis Davis), perfume model (Ursula Menzel), first model (Susan Shute), second model (Edie Baskin), third model (Gabrielle), fourth model (Giny Kaneen), mermaid (Susan Henning), first motorcycle cop (Morgan Windbell) second motorcycle cop (Benjie Nacroft).

(*Running time*: 89 mins)

Charro! (1968)

Studio: National General Picture Corporation

Producer/director/Screenplay: Charles Marquis Warren

Associate producer/Assistant director: Dink Templeton

Executive Producer: Harry Caplan

Story: Frederic Louis Fox – based on the novel *Charro!* by Harry Whittington.

Photography: Ellsworth Fredericks ASC

Editor: Al Clark ACE

Music: Hugo Montenegro

Art direction: James Sullivan

Cast: Jess Wade (Elvis Presley), Tracy Winters (Ina Balin), Vince Hackett (Victor French), Sara Ramsey (Barbara Werle), Billy Roy (Solomon Sturgess), Marcie (Lynn Kellog), Gunner (James Sikking), Opie Keetch (Paul Brinegar), Heff (Harry Landers), Lieutenant Rivera (Tony Young), Sheriff Dan Ramsey (James Almanzar), Mody (Charles H. Gray), Lige (Rodd Redwing), Martin Tilford (Gary Walberg), Gabe (Duane Grey), Henry Carter (J. Edward McKinley), Jerome Selby (John Pickard), Will Joslyn (Robert Luster), Christa (Christa Lang), Barman Harvey (Robert Karnes)

(*Running time*: 98 mins)

The Trouble with Girls (And How to Get into it) (1968)

Studio: Metro-Goldwyn-Mayer
Director: Peter Tewksbury
Producer: Lester Welch
Screenplay: Arnold and Lois Peyser
Story: based on the novel *Chautauqua* by Day Keene and Dwight Babcock

Photography: Jacques Marquette ASC
Editor: George W. Brooks
Music: Billy Strange
Choreography: Jonathan Lucas
Art direction: George W. Davis and Edward Carfagno

Costumes Bill Thomas

Cast: Walter Hale (Elvis Presley), Charlene (Marlyn Mason), Nita Bix (Sheree North), Betty (Nicole Jaffe), Johnny (Edward Andrews), Mr Drewcolt (John Carradine), Mr Morality (Vincent Price), Carol (Anissa Jones), Maude (Joyce Van Patten), Willy (Pepe Brown), Harrison Wilby (Dabney Coleman), Mayor Gilchrist (Bill Zuckert), Mr Perper (Pitt Herbert), Clarence (Anthony Teague), constable (Med Flory), Mrs Gilchrist (Patsy Garrett).

(*Running Time*: 104 mins/UK 79 mins)

Change of Habit (1969)

Studio: Universal
Director: William Graham
Producer: Joe Connelly
Associate producer: Irving Paley
Screenplay: James Lee, S.S. Schweitzer and Eric Bercovici
Story: John Joseph and Richard Morris

Photography: Russell Metty ASC
Editor: Douglas Stewart
Music: William Goldenberg
Art direction: Alexander Golitzen and Frank Arrigo
Costumes: Helen Colvig

Cast: Dr John Carpenter (Elvis Presley), Sister Michelle (Mary Tyler Moore), Sister Irene (Barbara McNair), Sister Barbara (Jane Elliot), Mother Joseph (Leora Dana), Lieutenant Moretti (Edward Asner), the banker (Robert Emhardt), Father Gibbons (Regis Toomey), Rose (Doro Merande) Lily (Ruth McDevitt), Bishop Finley (Richard Carlson), Julio Hernandez (Nefti Millet), Amanda (Lorena Kirk), Desiree (Laura Figueroa), Miss Parker (Virginia Vincent), Colom (David Renard), Hawk (Ji-Tu Cumbaka)

(*Running time*: 93 mins)

Elvis – That's the Way it is (1970)

Studio: Metro-Goldwyn-Mayer
Director: Denis Sanders
Unit production manager: Dale Hutchinson
Photography: Lucien Ballard ASC
Editors: Henry Berman ACE and George Folsey jun.
Musical conductor: Joe Guercio

Elvis's Wardrobe: Bill Belew
Musicians with Elvis: James Burton, John Wilkinson, Charlie Hodge (guitar), Jerry Scheff (bass), Glen D. Hardin (piano) Ronnie Tutt (drums), Millie Kirkham, The Imperials Quartet, The Sweet Inspirations (vocals).

(*Running time*: 108 mins)

Elvis on Tour (1972)

Studio: Metro-Goldwyn-Mayer
Producer/Director: Pierre Adidge and Robert Abel
Associate producer: Sidney Levin
Photography: Robert Thomas
Editor: Ken Zemke
Musical conductor: Joe Guercio
Montage supervisor: Martin Scorsese
Elvis's Wardrobe: Bill Belew
Musicians with Elvis: James Burton (lead guitar), Charlie Hodge (guitar and vocal), Ronnie Tutt (drums), Glen D. Hardin (piano), John Wilkinson (rhythm guitar), Jerry Scheff (bass guitar), Kathy Westmoreland, The Sweet Inspirations, J.D. Sumner and The Stamps Quartet (vocals).
Research: Andrew W. Solt, Carole Kismaric, Jack Goelman
Assistants to Elvis: Vernon Presley, Joe Esposito, Jerry Schilling, Sonny West, Red West, James Caughley, Lamar Fike, Marvin Gamble.

(*Running time*: 93 mins)

All dates quoted refer to year of production.

Index